PostSecret

PostSecret

EXTRAORDINARY CONFESSIONS
FROM ORDINARY LIVES

COMPILED BY

Frank Warren

The right of Frank Warren to be identified as the author of this work has been asserted
by him in accordance with the Copyright, Designs and Patents Act 1988.

This edition first published in Great Britain in 2006 by
Orion Books
an imprint of the Orion Publishing Group Ltd
Orion House, 5 Upper St Martin's Lane,
London WC2H 9EA

10 9 8 7 6 5 4 3 2

A CIP catalogue record for this book is available
from the British Library.

ISBN: 978 0 75287 598 9

Designed by Richard Ljoenes

Printed in Spain by Cayfosa-Quebecor

The Orion Publishing Group's policy is to use papers that are natural, renewable and recyclable and made from wood grown
in sustainable forests. The logging and manufacturing processes are expected to conform to the environmental regulations
of the country of origin.

Every effort has been made to fulfil requirements with regard to reproducing copyright material.
The author and publisher will be glad to rectify any omissions at the earliest opportunity.

www.orionbooks.co.uk

This book is dedicated to every person who faced their secret on a postcard, released it into a mailbox, and bravely shared it with me, the world, and themselves.

—Frank

The Most Trusted Stranger in America

I met Frank Warren after seeing PostSecret at Artomatic—a Washington, D.C., arts festival. As a practicing clinical psychologist and art gallery owner with an eye toward the psychological and healing aspects of art, I was looking for new artists to show at my gallery. At the PostSecret installation, I saw three rows of postcards, each with a taboo thought, each with artistic images, carefully clipped to display wires. There hung dozens of anonymous secrets on public display.

"This is one of the most amazing projects I have ever seen," I said to my husband. "I've got to have this in the gallery." Without pausing, my husband looked at me with worry. "Do you think the person who is doing this is safe?" he asked.

Frank, it turns out, is very safe. A father, husband, and business owner, he has no formal art background or training and refers to himself as an "accidental artist." Four years ago Frank experienced an emotional crisis in his life. Developing a passion for postcard art projects was how he worked through it. It became his personal experience of healing through art. He doesn't like to think too much about the origin or meanings of his postcard art works. He likens it to trying to understand why a joke is funny; the magic may be lost in the attempt to analyze it. He does know this: While at camp, when he was nine years old, he wrote a postcard to his family. He arrived home before the card did. Receiving it seemed magical and felt deeply meaningful to him. He had intercepted a message from himself as he had been days earlier. As he considers the event now, he believes those themes of home, understanding our changing identities, and self-communication held long-term inspiration.

Why is PostSecret so appealing? It is because Frank has tapped into the universal stuff of being human—the collective, often unconscious level of existence that defies age, culture, gender, economics, and so on. From this universal level come great and timeless works of art: theater, music, dance, visual art, and literature. At this universal level lie the depths of spirituality: mythological tales, sacred text, and ritual. Also from this universal level comes direct access to healing and personal transformation. Although in Western cultures we act as though there is a separation, there is no separation of the arts from spirituality or healing.

By participating in PostSecret, we all are invited into that collective level to become artists—free to explore and share private aspects of ourselves creatively, both through writing and through the alternative language of visual art. Whether we are PostSecret creators or viewers, we are affected and changed by experiencing the creative process and interacting with the resulting works of art.

The project also invites us into the collective level to heal ourselves, healing that has several characteristics similar to psychotherapy. For example, the prominent themes in PostSecret mirror some of the reasons people are drawn to psychotherapy: seeking relief from suffering; sharing painful experiences (especially concerning difficulties in relationships or feelings of isolation); expressing shame and anxiety about aspects of self that are difficult to face; and admitting one's impulses, fears, and fantasies. Although many of the secrets are about psychological pain, the grist for the mill in psychotherapy, others are hopeful, optimistic, or even humorous. Hope and humor are certainly important aspects of the psychotherapeutic process as well.

In PostSecret, by being asked to share a secret, we are invited to journey into our depths, perhaps into the unconscious mind, beneath the level of our awareness at the moment. Perhaps we venture into the preconscious where our secrets are already on the verge of awareness and emergence, or maybe into the conscious, where our secrets are being held back, ready to be let out under the right circumstances. As in psychotherapy, we are provided with a projective screen onto which anything can be placed and viewed. In this case, it is the postcard.

Also, as in psychotherapy, there is an action element in PostSecret. There is something that we can do—fill out the postcard. Reading the postcards is also a form of taking action. Something might change. There is hope. My patients often tell me how much better they feel after making the phone call to arrange for the first therapy appointment or after the first psychotherapy session. They have taken action toward healing; they feel hopeful that their lives will improve.

Both in psychotherapy and in PostSecret, the goal is to bring experience to conscious awareness and to express what is deepest inside and not have it be the end of the world. The goal is to make inner experience concrete by placing it outside the self. This exercise gives us the potential and the opportunity for self-reflection, for self-acceptance, for increased understanding about the self, and for healing and personal growth.

PostSecret is even briefer than the briefest of psychotherapies. The healing experience in PostSecret is bite-size, manageable. One postcard, one shared aspect of self, the secret, shared in a structured way, shared as part of an art project that may slip quietly under the radar of the psychological defenses. Release the secret onto the card, then release the card to Frank by mailing it, and notice what happens inside.

Albeit an anonymous process, PostSecret also shares some characteristics of the healing relationship with psychotherapy. At the foundation of psychotherapy is relationship, no matter the technique. It is about one human being expressing authentic caring and concern for another, offering comfort, witness, acceptance, assistance, and hope. When you send the postcard to Frank, he is on the other end to receive it. The same person who has offered us an opportunity to share has taken an interest in us and is there for us, unconditionally.

In PostSecret, art and healing are one, brilliantly condensed into the elegant simplicity of filling out a postcard. All for the price of a 37-cent stamp.

Frank told me recently, "There are times when I feel like this project has chosen me and not the other way around, and at times it feels like it may have picked the wrong person." Or maybe it has found exactly the right person.

Anne C. Fisher, Ph.D.
August 2005

Anne C. Fisher is a former classical ballerina, a practicing dance therapist, and a clinical psychologist.
The Anne C. Fisher Fine Art Gallery is located in Georgetown in Washington D.C.

SHARE A SECRET

You are invited to anonymously contribute a secret to a group art project. Your secret can be a regret, fear, betrayal, desire, confession or childhood humiliation. Reveal *anything* - as long as it is true and you have never shared it with anyone before.

Steps:
   Take a postcard, or two.
   Tell your secret anonymously.
   Stamp and mail the postcard.

Tips:
   Be brief – the fewer words used the better.
   Be legible – use big, clear and bold lettering.
   Be creative – let the postcard be your canvas.

SEE A SECRET
www.postsecret.com

PostSecret
13345 Copper Ridge Rd
Germantown, Maryland
20874-3454

place
postage
here

In November 2004, I printed 3,000 postcards inviting people to share a secret with me: something that was true, something they had never told anyone. I handed out these cards at subway stations, I left them in art galleries, and I slipped them between the pages of library books. Then, slowly, secrets began to find their way to my mailbox.

After several weeks I stopped passing out postcards but secrets kept coming. Homemade postcards made from cardboard, old photographs, wedding invitations, and other personal items artfully decorated arrived from all over the world. Some of the secrets were written in Portuguese, French, German, Hebrew, and even Braille.

One of the first PostSecrets I received looked like nothing more than a worn postcard filled with two shopping lists. But squeezed into the corner was a soulful admission, "I am still struggling with what I've become."

Like fingerprints, no two secrets are identical, but every secret has a story behind it. From the clues on this card, I imagined that this person had an internal struggle about sharing the secret. It was so difficult that they tried to use up the postcard as a shopping list, twice. But the urge to reconcile with a painful personal truth was so strong that they were ultimately able to find the courage to share it.

Secrets have stories; they can also offer truths. After seeing thousands of secrets, I understand that sometimes when we believe we are keeping a secret, that secret is actually keeping us. A New Zealander recently wrote the following about what they had learned from the PostSecret project, "The things that make us feel so abnormal are actually the things that make us all the same."

I invite you to contemplate each of the shared secrets in these pages: to imagine the stories behind the personal revelations and to search for the meaning they hold. As you read these postcards you may not only be surprised by what you learn about others, but also reminded of your own secrets that have been hiding. That is what happened to me.

After reading one particular PostSecret, I was reminded of a childhood humiliation—something that happened to me more than thirty years ago. I never thought of it as a secret, yet I had never told anyone about it. From a memory that felt fresh, I chose my words carefully and expressed my secret on a postcard. I shared it with my wife and daughter. The next day, I went to the post office, and physically let it go into a mailbox. I walked away feeling lighter.

I like to think that this project germinated from that secret I kept buried for most of my life. At a level below my awareness, I needed to share it, but I was not brave enough to do it alone. So I found myself inviting others at galleries and libraries to first share their secrets with me. And when their postcards found me, I was able to find the courage to identify my secret and share it too.

We all have secrets: fears, regrets, hopes, beliefs, fantasies, betrayals, humiliations. We may not always recognize them but they are part of us—like the dreams we can't always recall in the morning light.

Some of the most beautiful postcards in this collection came from very painful feelings and memories. I believe that each one of us has the ability to discover, share, and grow our own dark secrets into something meaningful and beautiful.

—Frank

i don't know WHICH ONE
to send in.

Cupulonimbus m
2004

Altocumulus castellanus

37 USA

37 USA

Post secret
13345 Copper Ridge Ro
Germantown, MD
20874-3454

5

my secret is...

I want to be a Outlaw Biker

I can't think of a secret.
Except —
I don't think I'm interesting enough to have a secret.

POSTSECRET
13345 COPPERRIDGE RD
GERMANTOWN,
    MARYLAND
USA 20874-3454

20874/3454

I found these
stamps ⟶
as a child, and I

have been
waiting all my
life to have someone
to send them to.
I never did have
someone.

Post Secret
13345 Copper Rid R
Germantown, MD
20874-3454

SOMETIMES
i
WISH THAT i
WAS
BLIND,
JUST SO i
WOULDN'T HAVE
TO LOOK
AT MYSELF
EVERYDAY
in THE MIRROR.

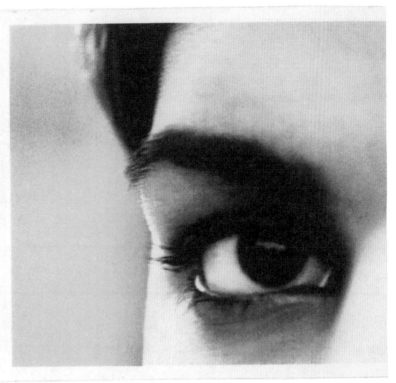

I think women who don't wear makeup..

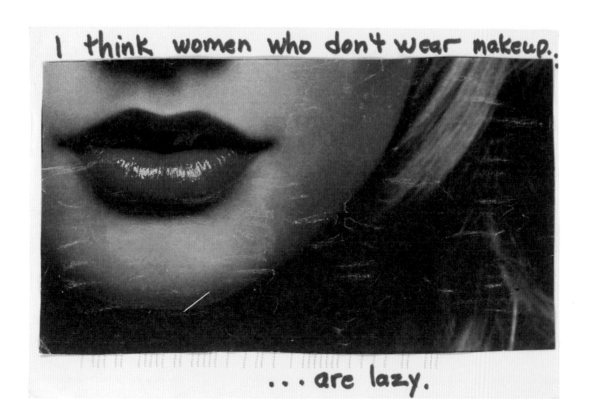

...are lazy.

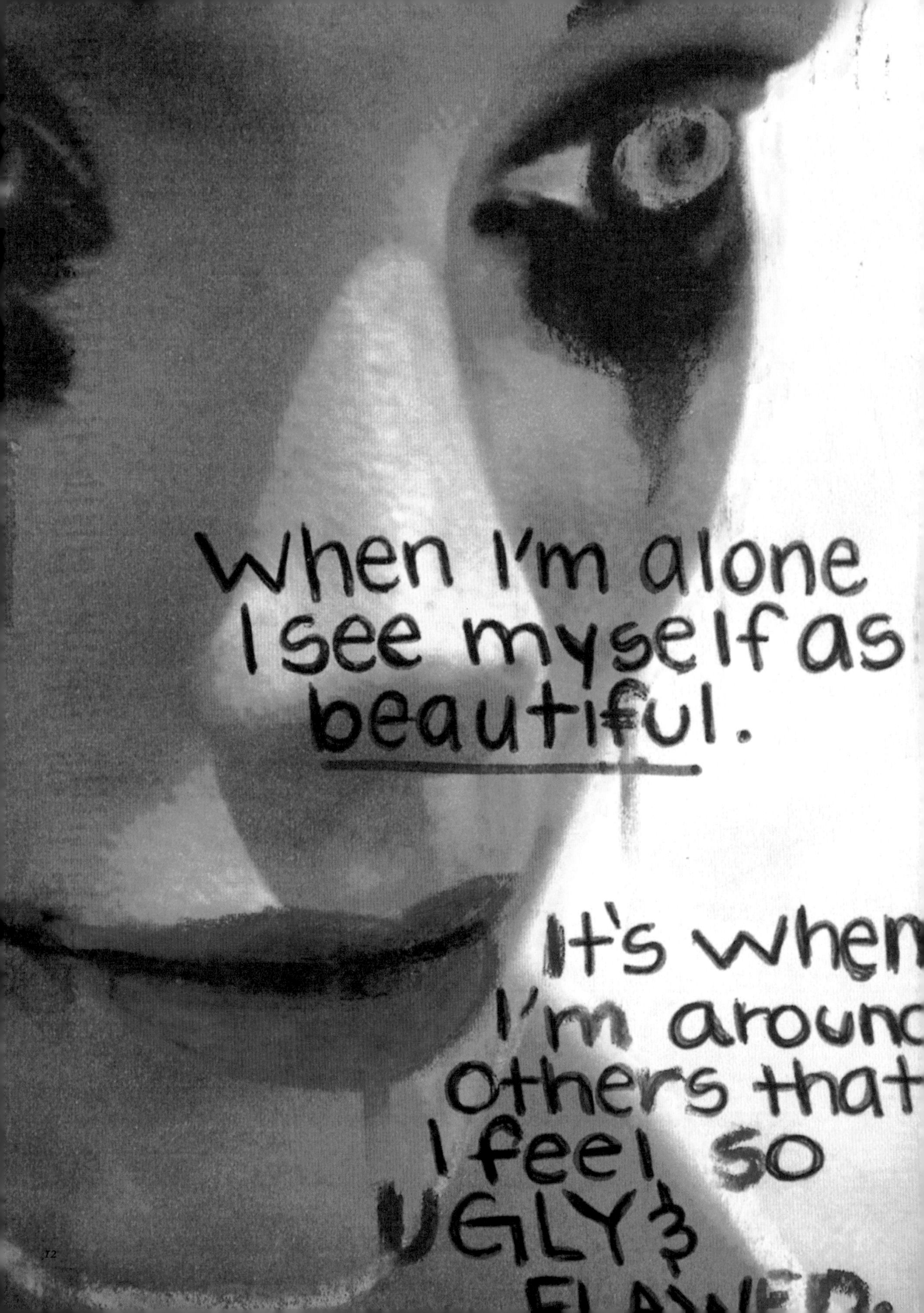

When I'm alone
I see myself as
beautiful.

It's when
I'm around
others that
I feel so
UGLY &
FLAWED.

I envy
the willpower
of
anorexics.

13

som

I PUT C
OTHER
PARKIN

etimes

OINS IN
PEOPLE'S
METERS

I

don't

know.

what

I

want

but

I

don't

want

this....

16

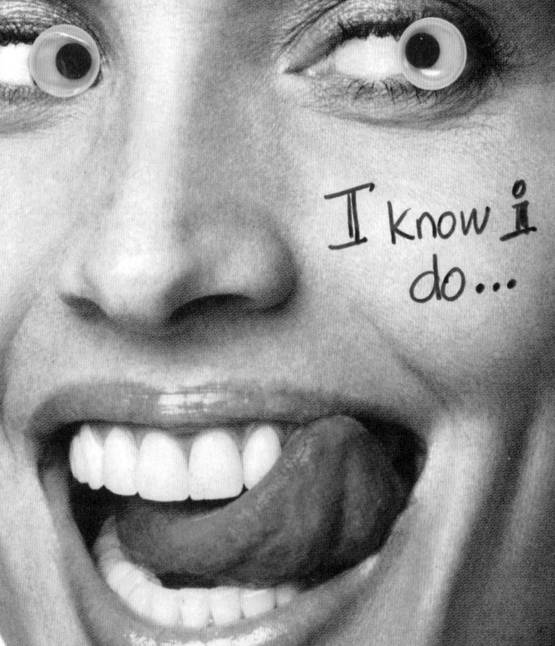

"There are two kin
those we keep fro
we hide from our

ds of secrets:
m others and those
elves."

—Frank

When I was in the Fourth Grade, a new kid moved into our neighborhood.

He was a charismatic leader who quickly became popular.

Soon after, he convinced two of my friends to pin me to the ground and hold open my eyelids.

They took turns spitting into my eyes.

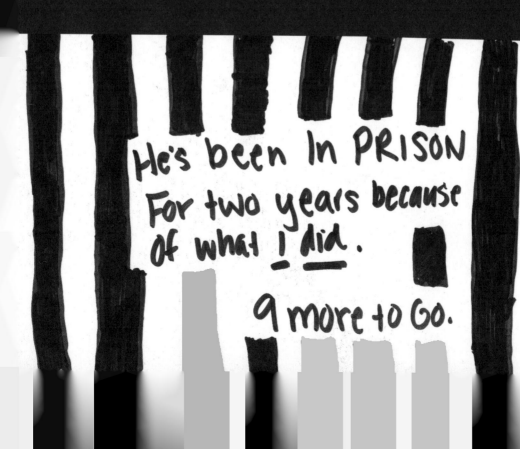

He's been In PRISON For two years because of what I did.

9 more to Go.

PEOPLE T

STOPP 
L

... but I've j
better at

HINK I'VE

ED

YING

ust gotten

it

I AM HOME-
LESS AND
NO ONE
(NOT EVEN
MY FAMILY)
KNOWS ABOUT IT.

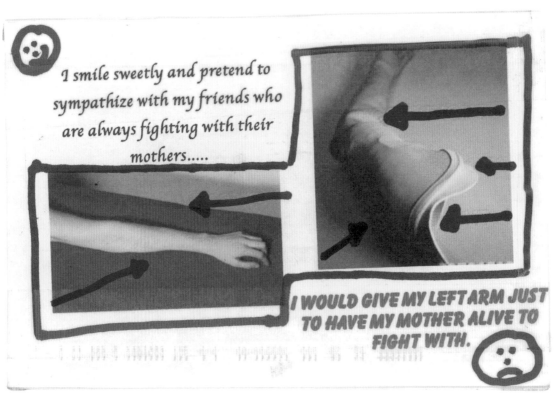

I smile sweetly and pretend to sympathize with my friends who are always fighting with their mothers.....

I WOULD GIVE MY LEFT ARM JUST TO HAVE MY MOTHER ALIVE TO FIGHT WITH.

I'm JEALOUS of her baby...

I Feel Guilty

All The Time

I waste office supplies because I hate my boss.

MESSAGE

Message For

from

number

date

I save all the staples I pull out at work.

they're in a box in my desk.

it weighs over a pound and a half.

I USED TO FERTILIZE A RING IN OUR LAWN EVERY TIME I MOWED IT.

IT GREW.

MY PARENTS still think it was ALIENS.

every morning

I go to work

hoping she'll say

"I Quit"

57 + 375 = 432

628 + 56 = 684

I am a successful, college-educated, 50-year-old businesswoman.

I still need to count with my fingers to add.

785.95
+ 128.24
+ 887.67

1801.86

There is a skittle on the bathroom floor at my job. Every time I go pee, I am tempted to eat it.

There is also a chocolate kiss under my desk. Its been there since I started, 1 1/2 years ago. I still might eat it.

Everyone thinks I do it to make people stare...

but really, it's to keep them from looking too closely

...It doesn't stop Me from wondering what they do see.

Post Secret
13345 Copper
Ridge Road
Germantown, MD
20874-3454

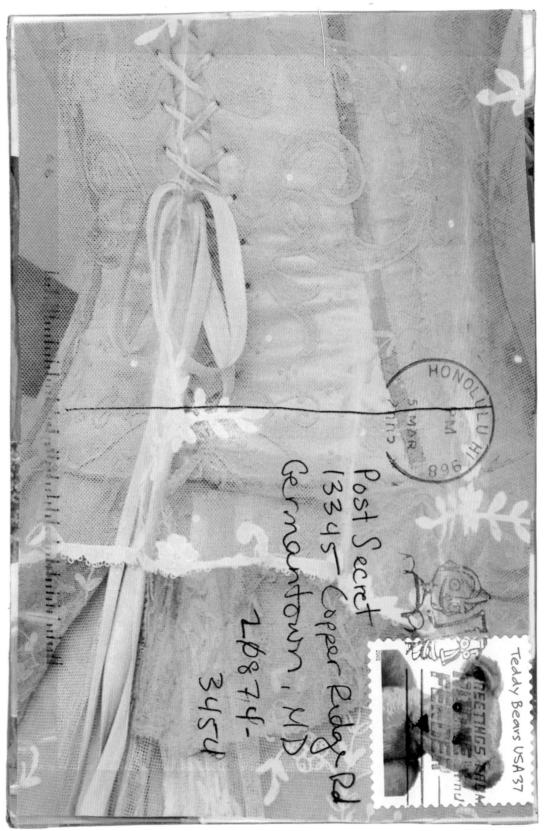

Post Secret
13345 Copper Ridge Rd
Germantown, MD
20874-
3450

Teddy Bears USA 37

(Back): *I married someone I don't love because I wanted to wear the dress.*

I'VE

ALWA

WANT

TO F

A BA

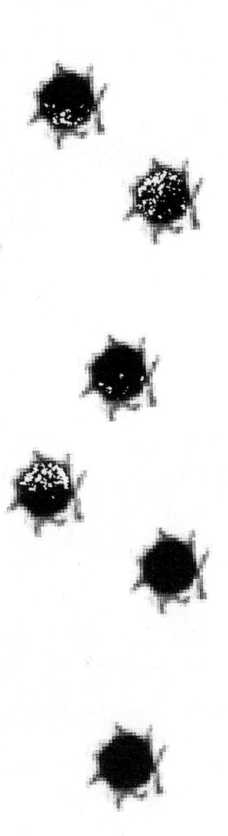

I DONT LIKE IT WHEN
MY HUSBAND LOOKS INTO MY

WHEN WE HAVE SEX. HE MIGHT
SEE MY SECRET.

MY FATHER DIED WHEN I WAS 12
I COULDN'T CRY

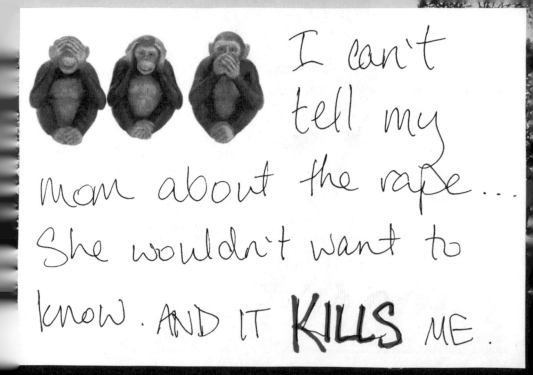

I can't tell my mom about the rape... She wouldn't want to know. AND IT **KILLS** ME.

I became a COP so I could try to STOP myself. It's not working...

I'm happy
and lucky
but I've never
told anyone.

I'm terrified of

not existing.

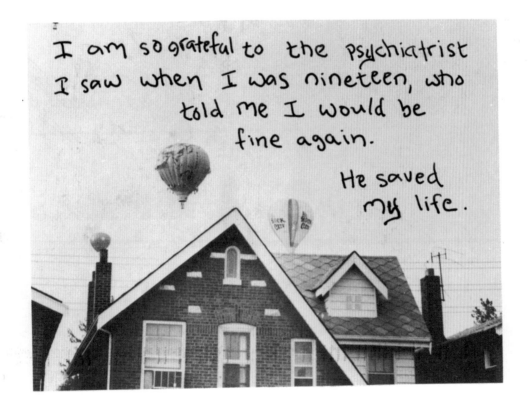

I am so grateful to the psychiatrist
I saw when I was nineteen, who
told me I would be
fine again.

He saved
my life.

LETTER SCORE

LETTER SCORE

DOUBLE LETTER SCORE

TRIPLE LETTER SCORE

TRIPLE LETTER SCORE

DOUBLE LETTER SCORE

DOUBLE LETTER SCORE

S₁ I₁ D₂ E₁

DOUBLE LETTER SCORE

DOUBLE LETTER SCORE

It really bothers me to admit this. It freaks me out.

I AM NOT A BIGOT!

I LOVE PEOPLE

i am a good person.

But I think Hitler was sexy.

44

When I was young teenager I used to babysit my next door neighbours so when their two sons were asleep I would go into their bedroom and through their bedside drawers and through a packet of condoms I've a pin through the middle of each of them and these days my neighbour tells them another years of babysitting!

When I'm mad at my husband....

...I put boogers in his soup.

I'm really scared of losing all of my weight because then I will be forced to face my fear of men and have no where to hide

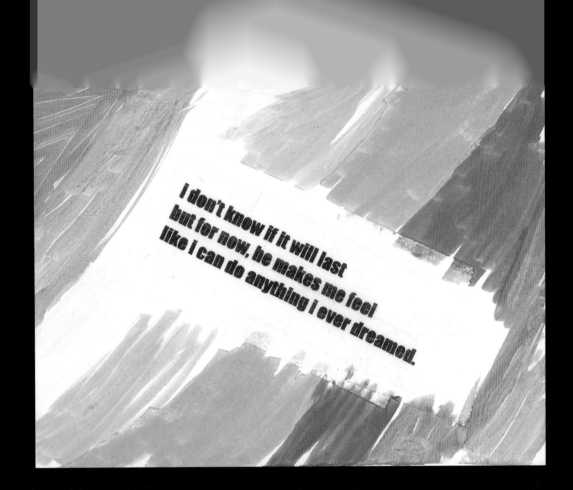

i don't know if it will last
but for now, he makes me feel
like i can do anything i ever dreamed.

I WILL
NEVER,
STOP
LOVING
HER

i fear that
i'm going to
be alone for
the rest of
my life.....

and i don't
want to have
to settle
in order
not to be.

I HAVE FINALLY SPOKEN MY SECRET
OUT LOUD

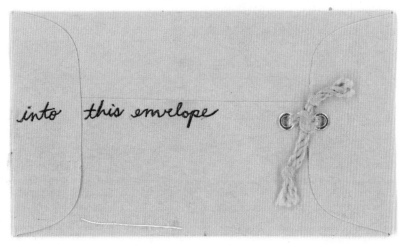

into this envelope

AND SEALED IT FOREVER.

Sometimes I want to run away from home. (I'm 38 married with a child.)

(Back): *I steal small things from my friends to keep memories of how much I love them.*

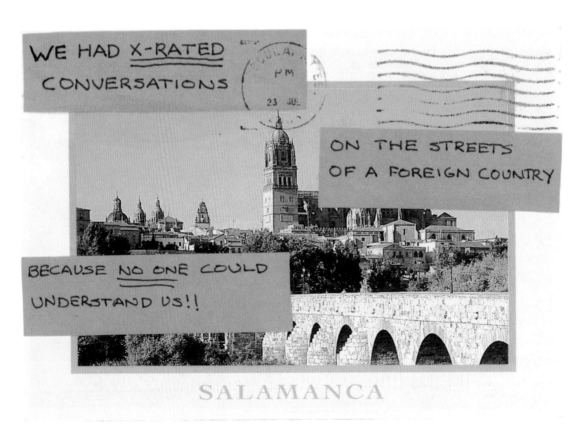

if i had a
million dollars,
i would give
it all away
for one more
day with her
like it used to
be in the
beginning.

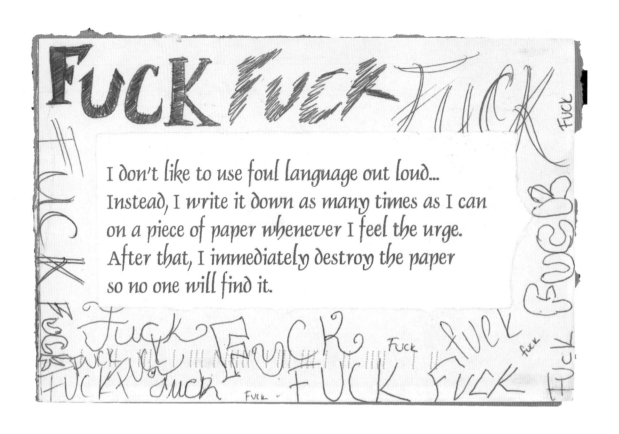

I don't like to use foul language out loud...
Instead, I write it down as many times as I can
on a piece of paper whenever I feel the urge.
After that, I immediately destroy the paper
so no one will find it.

I ONCE PUT HAIR IN MY PASTA AT A RESTAURANT WHEN I DECIDED THAT I WANTED FRIES INSTEAD...

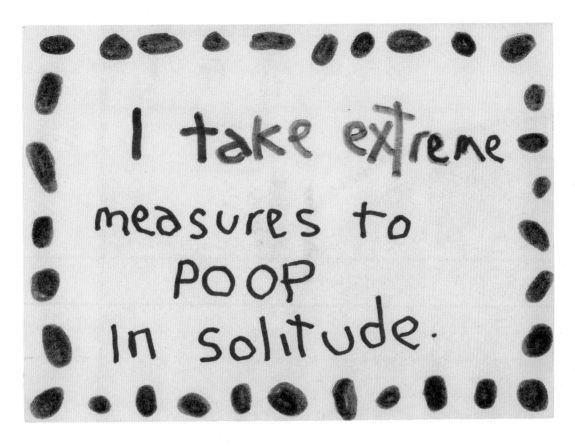

I take extreme· measures to POOP In solitude.

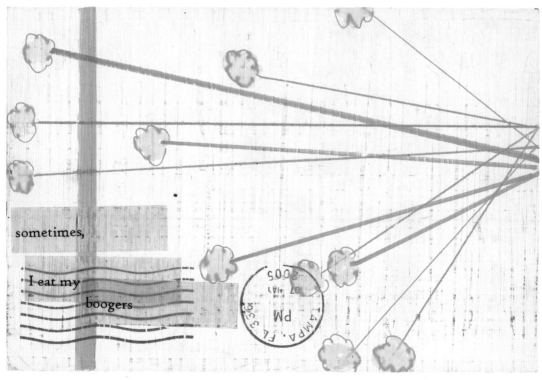

sometimes,

I eat my

boogers

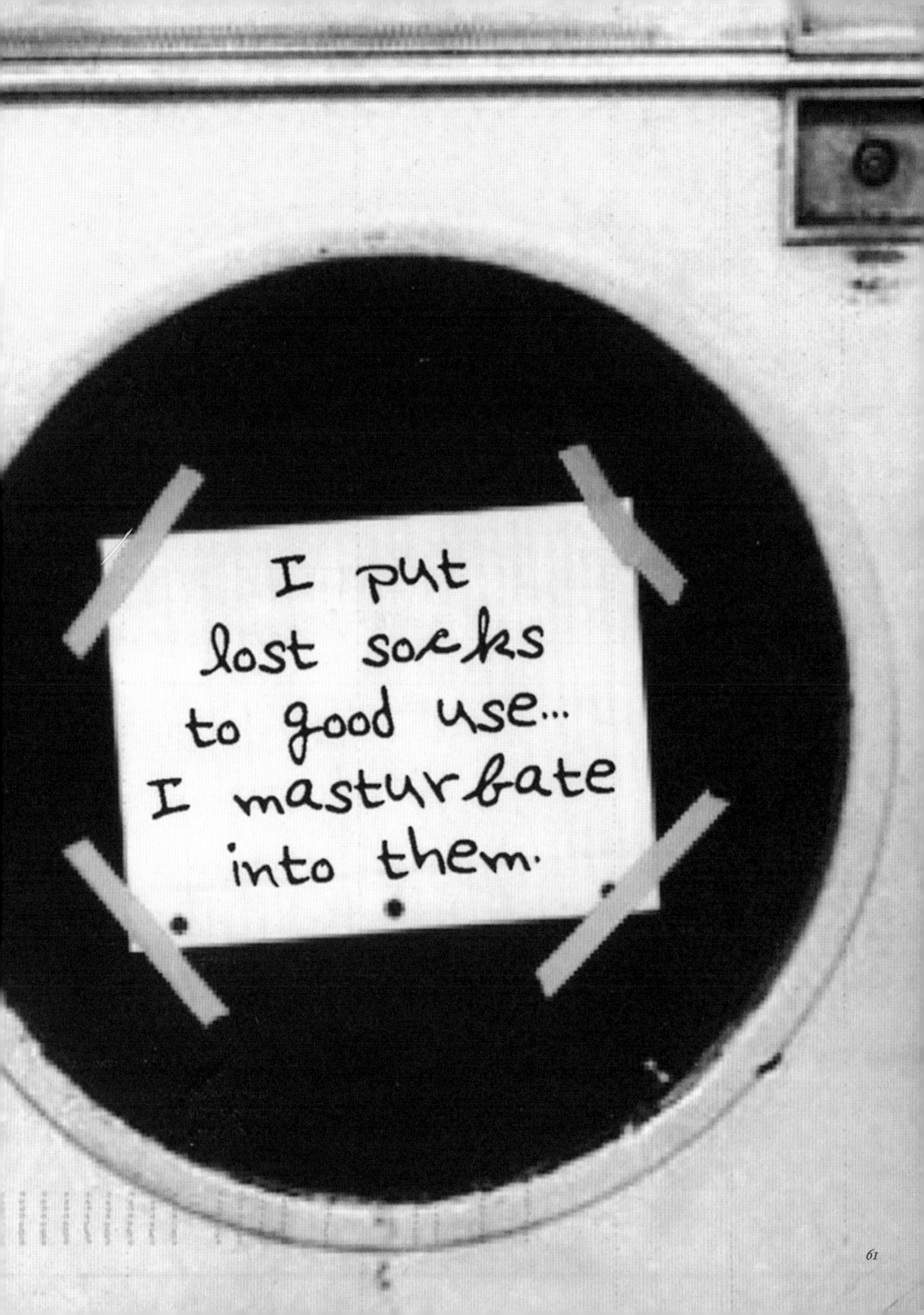
I put
lost socks
to good use...
I masturbate
into them.

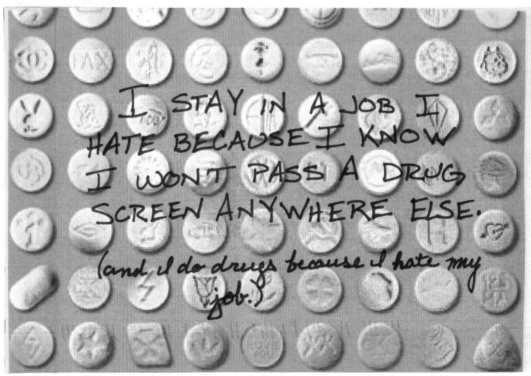

my dad died when i was 9 and i
convinced myself he'd faked his own
death for some reason (undercover
agent, chased by mob, etc.) and that
he'd come back someday.

when i was 12 i found out from my
psychiatrist that this is a pretty
stupid idea

i'm 25 now

i still wonder when it'll be safe
for him to come out of hiding and
find me

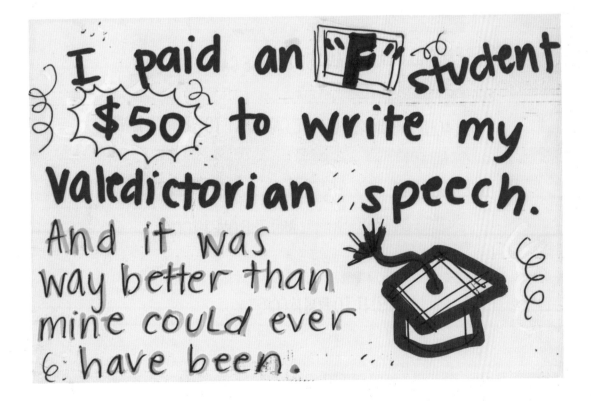

I paid an "F" student $50 to write my valedictorian speech. And it was way better than mine could ever have been.

I want to be a DOCTOR but I dont think I'll make it to med school.

I GOT A PARKING CITATION AND SO DID THE CAR NEXT TO ME.

I REPLACED THE TICKET ON THE CAR NEXT TO ME WITH MINE.

MY TICKET GOT PAID.

AND THE ONE I TOOK?

I MAILED IT TO POSTSECRET.

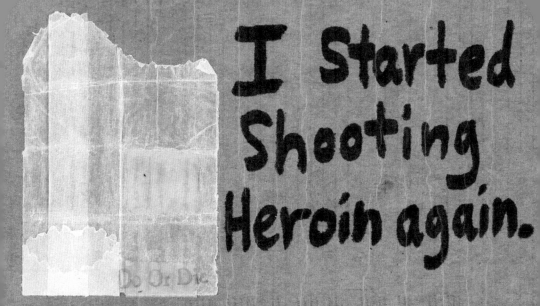

I Started Shooting Heroin again.

Do Or Die

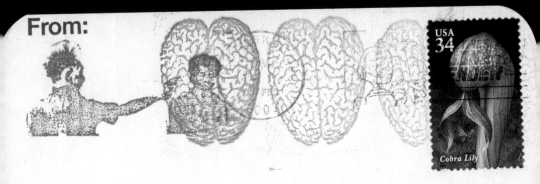

From:

USA 34
Cobra Lily

TO: POSTSECRET
13345 COPPER RIDGE ROAD
GERMANTOWN, MD.
20874

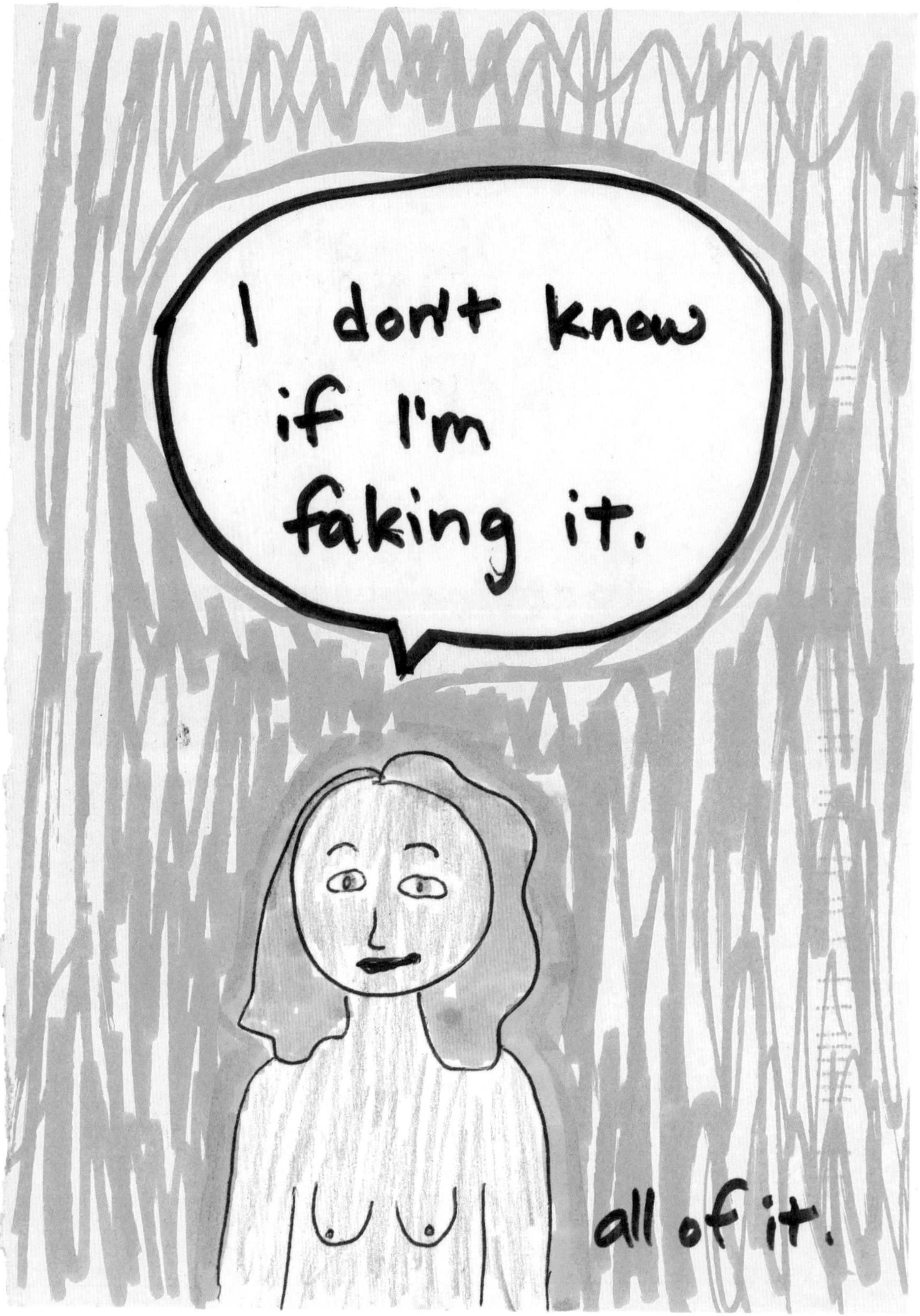
I don't know if I'm faking it.
all of it.

Sometimes after dark my friends and I strip down to our bras and panties and run around our local park, swing on the swings and feel so **free**. Afterwards I sketch it.

We call it **Liberation**.

I tell people that I don t believe in God,

when really,

I just refuse to worship a god

that would let my grandfather

HURT me

like he did.

I wished
on a dandelion
for my husband
to die.

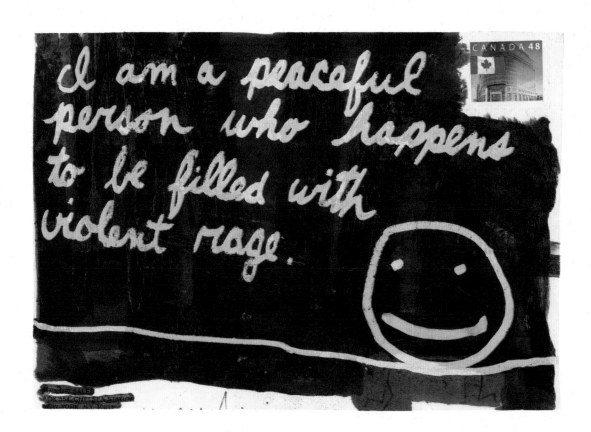

"Sometimes ju
sharing a pair
relieve some o

st the act of

ful secret can

of the pain."

—Maryland

Every thing that I told her →

I pray for this girl to flunk the ivy league and become a gas attendant

Refund

69 Other payments from: **a** ☐ Form 2439 **b** ☐ Form 4136 **c** ☐ Form 8885 . | **69**

70 Add lines 63, 64, 65a, and 66 through 69. These are your **total payments** . . . ▶

Direct deposit?
See page 54 and fill in 72b, 72c, and 72d.

71 If line 70 is more than line 62, subtract line 62 from line 70. This is the amount you **overpai**

72a Amount of line 71 you want **refunded to you** . . . ▶

▶ **b** Routing number | ▶ **c** Type: ☐ Checking ☐ Savings

▶ **d** Account number

73 Amount of line 71 you want **applied to your 2005 estimated tax** ▶ | **73**

Amount You Owe

74 **Amount you owe.** Subtract line 70 from line 62. For details on how to pay, see page 55 ▶

75 Estimated tax penalty (see page 55) . . . | **75**

Third Party Designee

Do you want to allow another person to discuss this return with the IRS (see page 56)? ☐ Ye

Designee's name ▶ | Phone no. ▶ ( ) | Personal ide number (PIN

Sign Here

Under penalties of perjury, I declare that I have examined this return and accompanying schedules and statements belief, they are true, correct, and complete. Declaration of preparer (other than taxpayer) is based on all information

Joint return?
See page 17.

Keep a copy for your records.

Your signature | *I. M. A. Crook* | Date | Your occupation

Spouse's signature. If a joint return, **both** must sign. | Date | Spouse's occupation

Paid Preparer's Use Only

Preparer's signature | Date | Check if self-employed ☐

Firm's name (or yours if self-employed) address, and ZIP code ▶ | EIN

Phone no

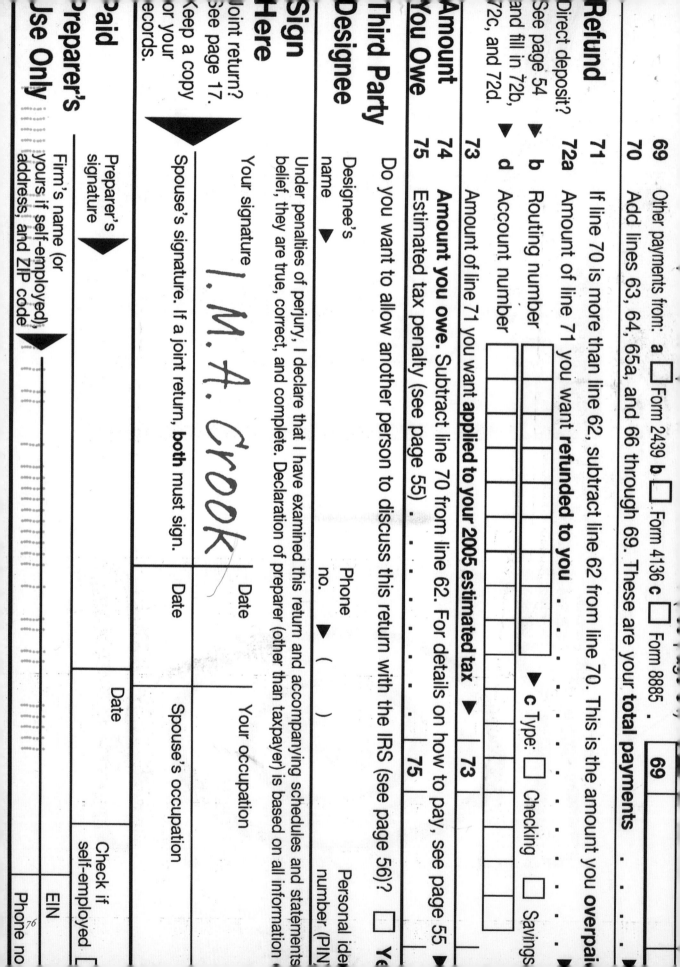

i am a
dot com
millionaire
but i told
my family
i missed
the bubble

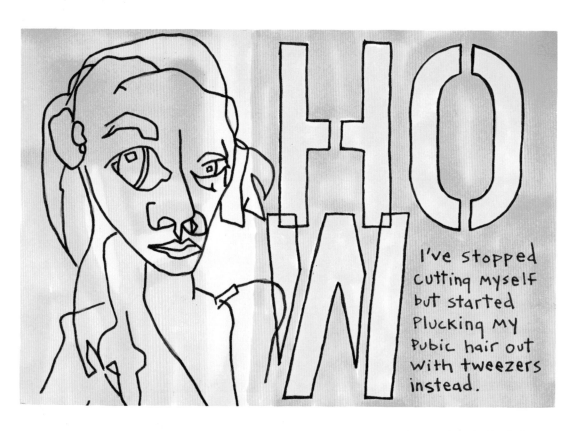

I believe that my dead grandmother watches me
with great disappointment every time I masturbate.

i considered
pressing statutory
rape charges.

just so he'd
regret breaking
my heart.

but then he'd never want
me back

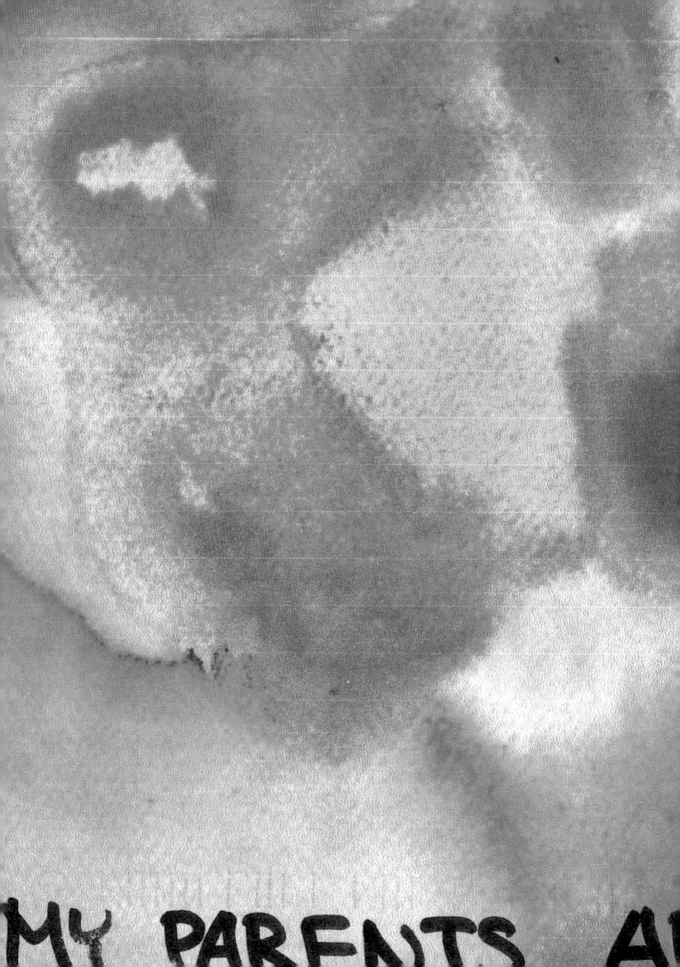

MY PARENTS A

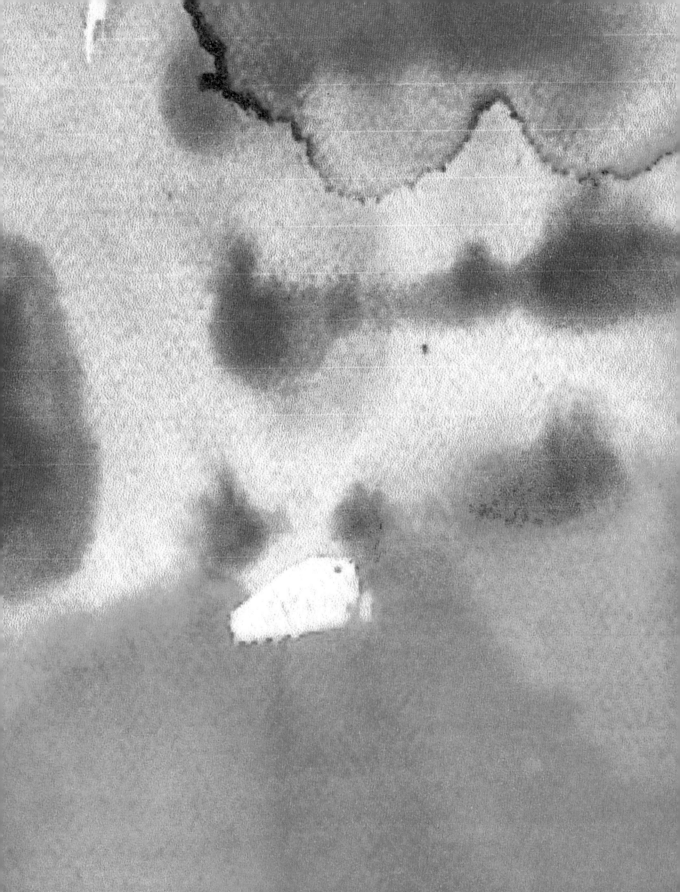

I tell everyone I'm **allergic** to cucumbers.

I'm not.

But now I'm scared to eat them.

Because I even told myself

I AM 100% SURE
I'D BE A RAPIST
. . .
if i'd been born a man.

Income

Attach Form(s) W-2 here,

Enclose, but do not attach, any payment.

1 Wages, salaries, and tips. This ~~s~~ Attach your Form(s) W-2.

2 Taxable interest. If the total is ov~~er~~

3 Unemployment compensation and (see page 13).

4 Add lines 1, 2, and 3. This is your

Income from teaching crea~~tive~~

a Total number of exempt~~ions~~

Income

Attach Form(s) W-2

7 Wages, salaries, tips, et~~c.~~

Income from writing creat~~ive~~

(See Instruction 20).

Print your numbers like this • 0 1 2 3 4 5 6 7 8 9 • not lik~~e~~

INCOME

1. Adjusted gross income from your federal return (See Instruct~~ion~~

1a. Wages, salaries and/or tips (See Instruction 11) . . . .

ADDITIONS TO INCOME (See Instruction 12)

uld be shown in box 1 of your Form(s) W-2.

$1,500, you cannot use Form 1040EZ.

laska Permanent Fund dividends

3

...justed gross income.

4

ive writing...$32,654.00

ns claimed.

Attach Form(s) W-2.

vely.................$0.00

Doll

1

1a

n 11)

I thought I was in love with him.

All of my life
people
have told me I'm not
special...
I'm very easy to
replace.

After 43 years it
has
finally sunk in.
I finally get it.

I hate people who "reply to all" on emails.

He Was Never that into Me, But I Let him Fake it For over a year!

Loving
You
Saved
My
Life.....

I always wait a few
days before returning e-mails
from my friends because
I don't want them to think
I have nothing better to do

I USED TO THINK THE RE

I make
sp

up fantasy
ories

because my real
life
SUCKS

And now my fantasy life
is starting to
suck, too.

(Back): *I got a restraining order against my ex... Now this is the only way I can tell him*

I WOULD GIVE
ANYTHING
FOR AN OPPORTUNITY
TO SHOW EVEN THE
SMALLEST KINDNESS
TO MY EX- WIFE

Free Matter
For The Blind

Postsecret
13345 Copper
Ridge Rd
Germantown MD
20874-3454

The love of my life is ugly.

My dog knew all my secrets, but one.
I put rat poison out back to get rid of a family of rats.
In around five days I had no more rats.
Around two weeks later, I had no dog.
I hope someone can learn from my mistake.
Max, I'm so sorry.
We miss you so, so much.

I'm afraid
that no one
will ever <u>love</u>
me ...
as much as
my dog does →

*CHARLIE

When people
I draw pict

cleveland

on Buses g

Disaster a

upset me

res of them

going to HELL

OHIO

100% PURE

EXTRA VIRGIN...

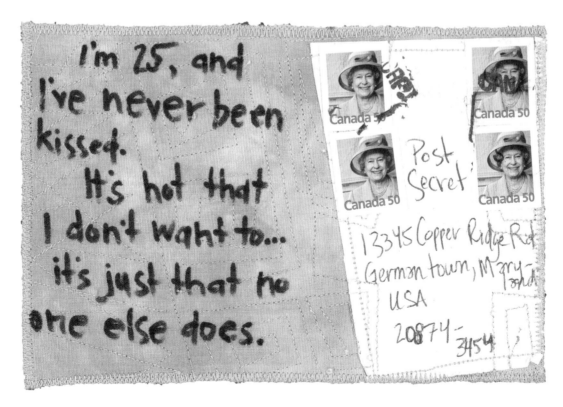

I'm 25, and I've never been kissed. It's not that I don't want to... it's just that no one else does.

Post Secret

13345 Copper Ridge Rd
Germantown, Mary-
land
USA
20874-
3454

Canada 50
Canada 50
Canada 50
Canada 50

21-VII-05

i still remember your birthday

Post Secret
13345 Cooper Ridge Rd.
Germantown, Maryland
20874-3454

(I still love you...)

And this↑is where I celebrated it this year.

I picked up this postcard and wrote a cute greeting on it and your

address. Then I remembered your new life without me and sent it to Post Secret instead.

LE PERE PINARD

RESTO
BAR
A
VINS
TAPAS

175 Ludlow Street NYC 10002   212.777.4917

I don't take my kids to the playground

because I don't like talking to the other moms.

HE WASN'T CHEATING ON YOU.

123 · Learn to listen. Opportunity sometimes knocks very softly.

BUT SINCE YOU CHOSE TO BLAME ME ANYWAY... HE WILL BE.

i wish my parents said I LoVe YoU... I can't remember hearing them say it... EVER!

i

se

the

WorD

NIGGER

I LOVE BLACK GIRLS

AND I AM WHITE
(It's OK!)

At the Artomatic exhibit, "It's OK!" was added to this card anonymously.

"Dear Frank,
How I wish I coulc
tell them that it's c
scared and angry a
It's part of being h

hug everyone and

k. It's ok to be

d hurt and selfish.

man."

—Ohio

When my fr

I discour

This is

really just w

fat

than

ends go on diets,

ge them.

ecause I

nt them to be

r

ne.

at a dozen

ONUTS

e sitting

I dreamt I was allergic to make-up.

Now I am.

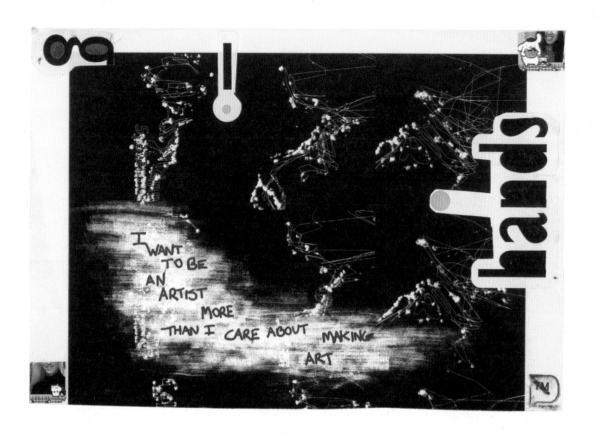

i give decaf to customers who are RUDE to me!

Decaf
Shots
Syrup
Milk
Custom
Drink

My SISTER and I EXPLORED EACH other sexually as CHILDREN. As the OLDER girl I feel GUILTY that I may have MOLESTED her.

Honestly, I'm glad your Uncle died, because he molested me that time in the 7th grade that I spent the night at your house... He told me that I liked it. I hope he likes it in his grave...

I had a CYST on my face THAT RUINED 7th AND 8th GRADE

Now, I LOVE IT Because IT MAKE ME DIFFERENT

-- because it won't get me in trouble --
--and real men have been too painful.

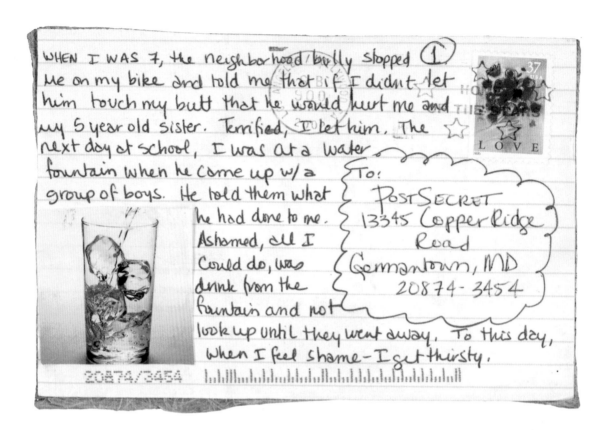

WHEN I WAS 7, the neighborhood bully stopped ①
Me on my bike and told me that if I didn't let
him touch my butt that he would hurt me and
my 5 year old sister. Terrified, I let him. The
next day at school, I was at a water
fountain when he come up w/ a
group of boys. He told them what
he had done to me.
Ashamed, all I
could do, was
drink from the
fountain and not
look up until they went away. To this day,
when I feel shame - I get thirsty.

To:
PostSecret
13345 Copper Ridge
Road
Germantown, MD
20874 - 3454

20874/3454

I believe that one
day I will like myself.

PostSecret
13345 Copper Ridge Rd
Germantown, MD
20874-3454

When I was 3 my dad liked me to brush his thick red hair. One day he asked and I said I didn't want to, I never saw him again.- he went away and then he died..

I am 65 & some days I still think it was my fault

JU
HE

I feel guilty about sometimes wishing that I didn't have children. I don't dare say it out loud for fear I might trigger something bad happening to them.

My parents think I'm checking my e-mail when I'm reading online erotica.

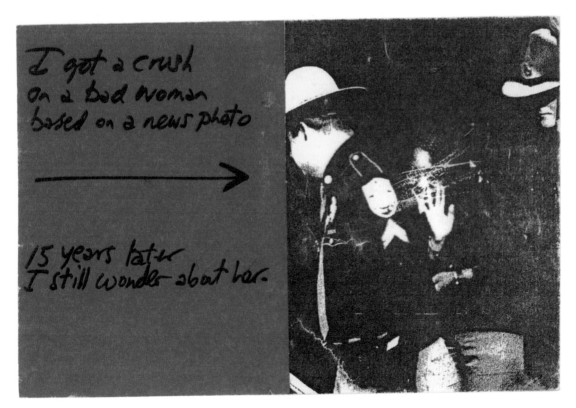

I love getti

It gives me
to be bitchy
and to

ng my period...

an excuse
and irritable
take naps.

i will never be

sexy?

enough.

Sometimes I cancel all of my appointments in a day. I tell everyone I'm sick... and pleasure myself all day.

I have so much fun - I'm exhausted - almost paralysed by pleasure.

The next day... I go back to work.

(Back): *When I was 12 my Mom joined the crowd of relatives who were laughing at me cause I couldn't carry a tune. I never whistled again.*

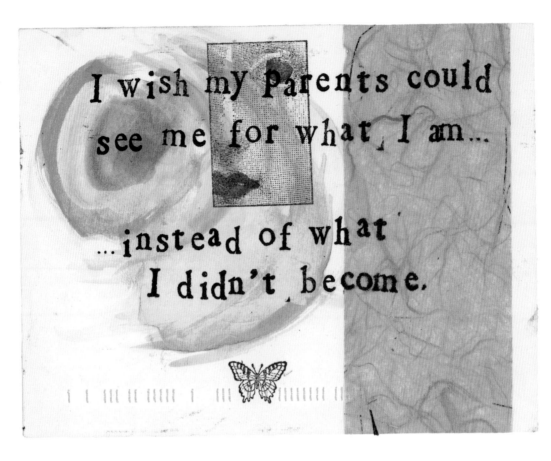

I wish my parents could see me for what I am...

...instead of what I didn't become.

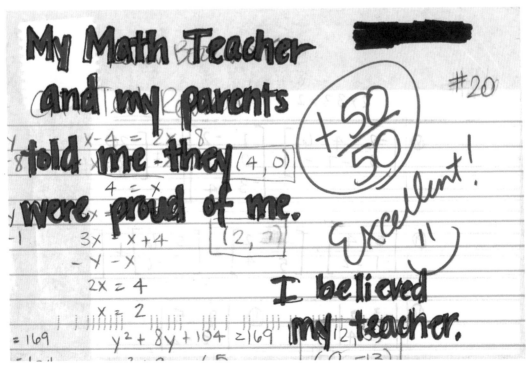

My Math Teacher and my parents told me they were proud of me.

I believed my teacher.

#20

+50/50

Excellent!

I love

If my

| | | | | | | ||| ||| |||| || | | |||| |

one

children.

|| | || ||| | | |||| |

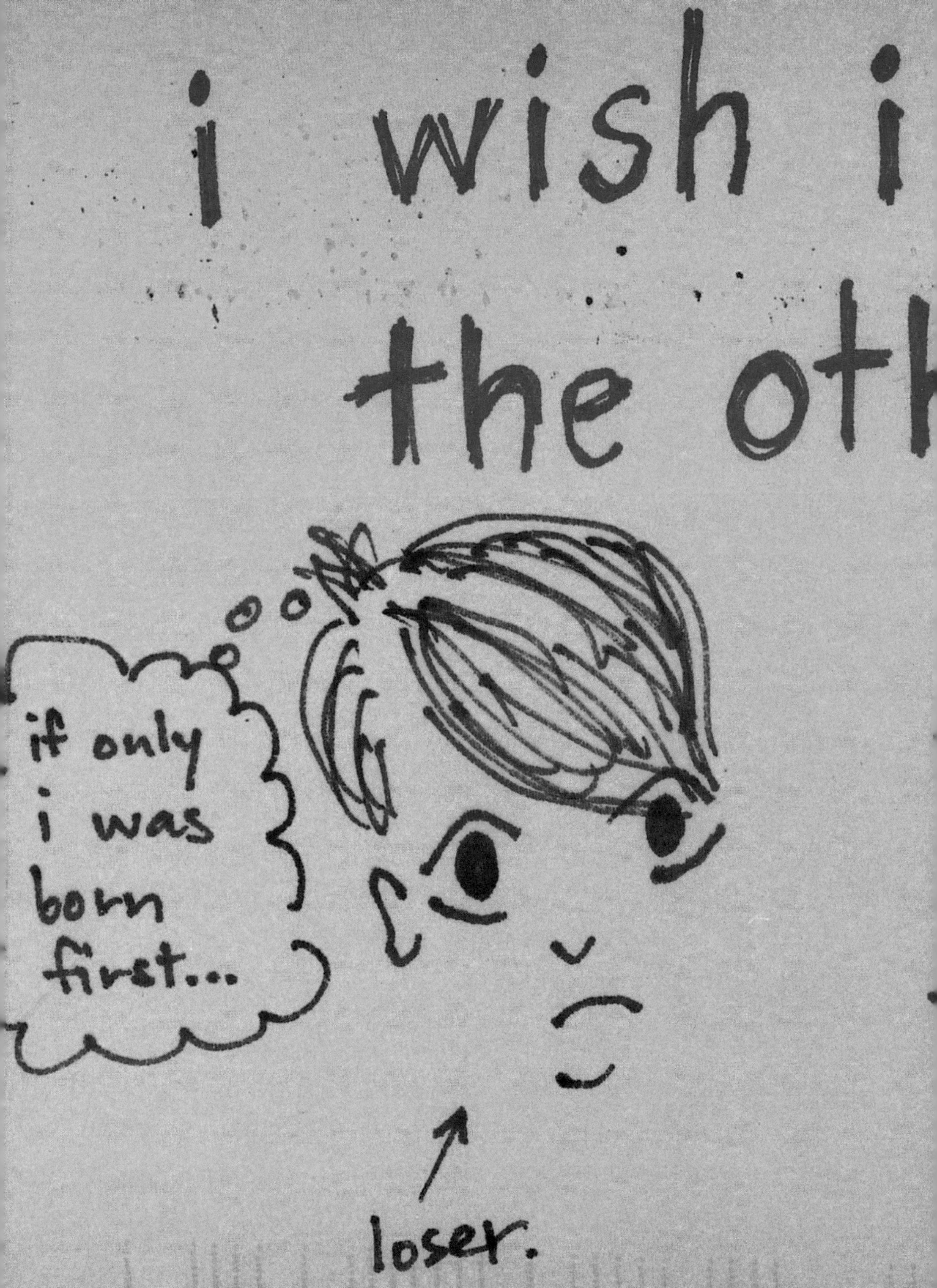

i wish i
the oth
if only i was born first...
loser.

was

er twin.

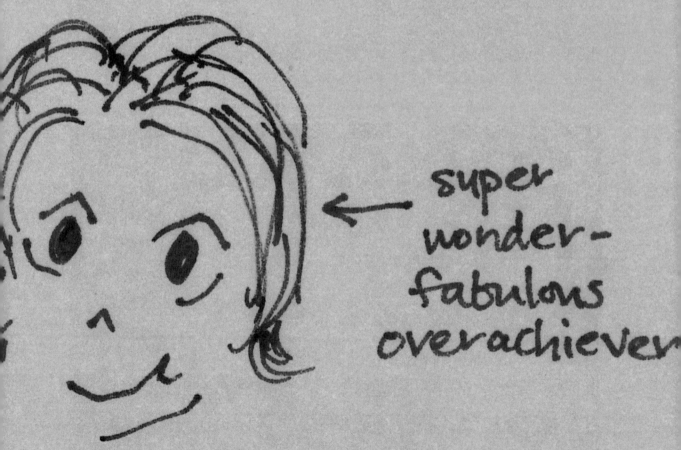

← super
wonder-
fabulous
overachiever

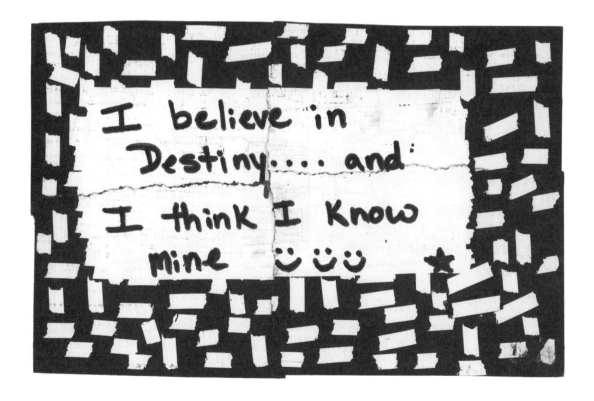

I wish my father
had forgiven me

while he was
still alive

everytime i approach an overpass,
i think how easy it would be to simply
turn the wheel ever so slightly to the
left and find peace, at long last...

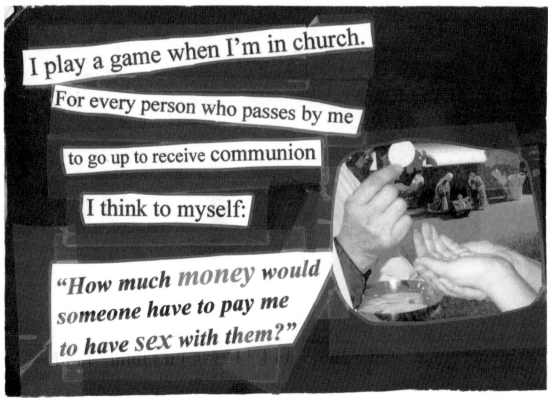

I miss feeling
close to God.

I Had gay sex
at church camp.

✝   ⍺

3 times.   ♡

what hurts more than losing you...

is knowing you're not fighting to keep me.

i'd gladly trade this car

to have a BIG penis.

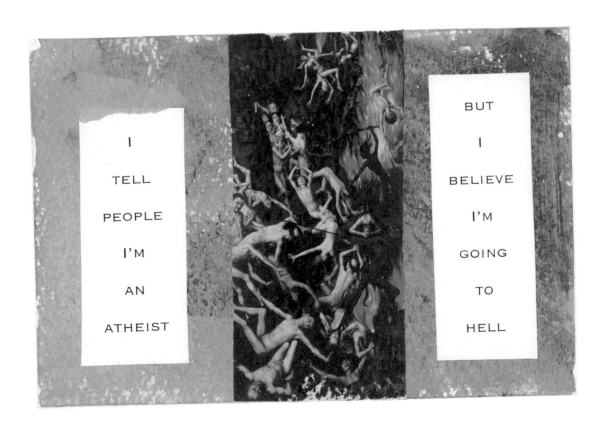

When i see an ugly bride, what i am really seeing is

a glimmer of hope for the future.

[maybe i will marry, someday.]

I THINK

PRIEST CASSOCKS ARE HOT

I CONVERTED BECAUSE
I THINK I LOOK
SEXY
IN A HEADSCARF

oath
———
i lied.

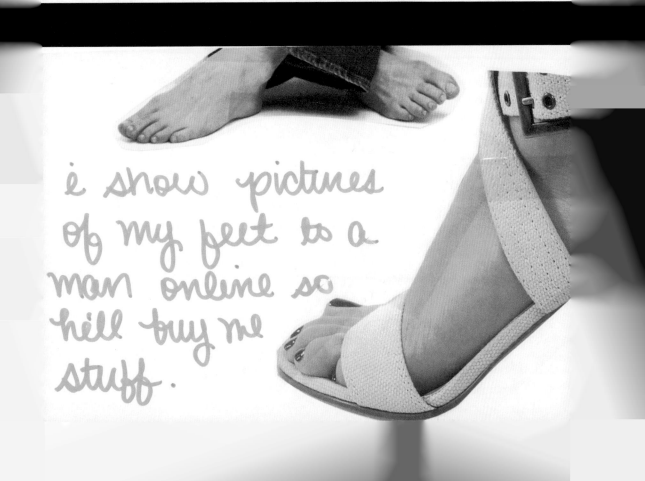

I DREAM: There is a Lover w[...]

who
will know that I'm
faking

さいはての海に浮かぶ、
漁場の標識　帆場瀬
Tom

"Dear Frank,
So many of my
without even se

secrets are there,

nding a card."

—Mexico

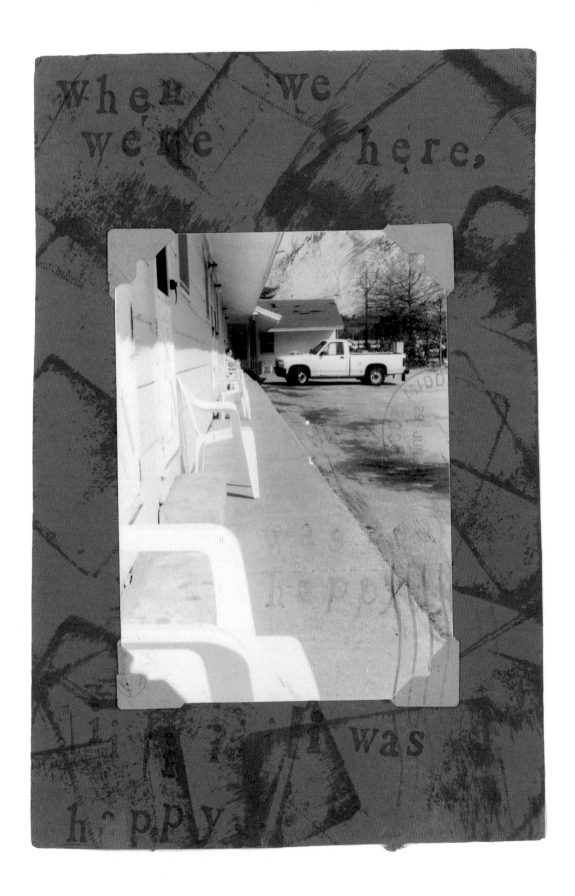

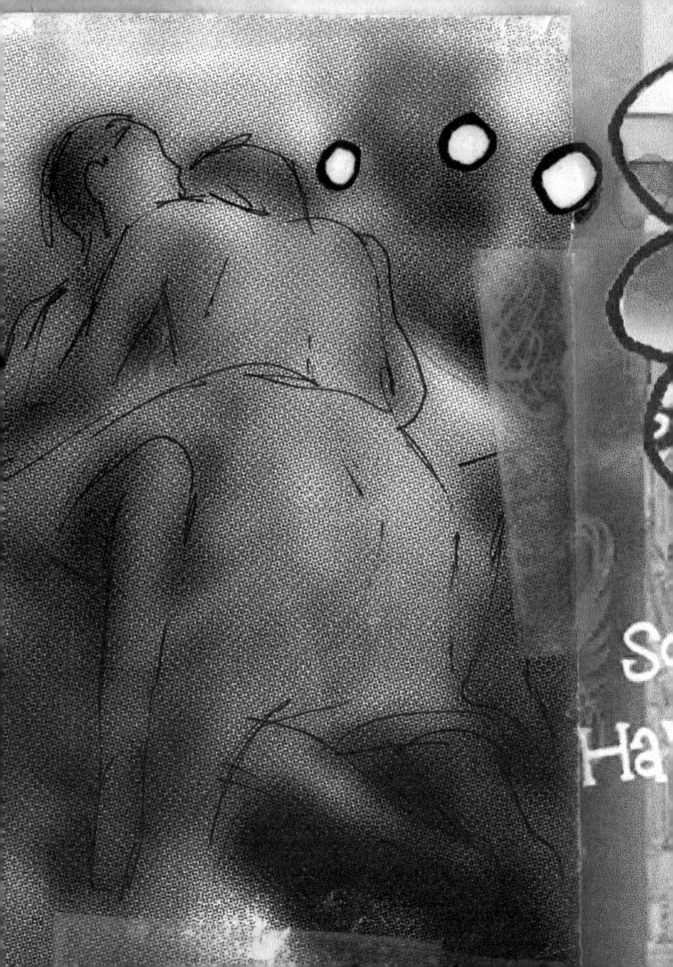

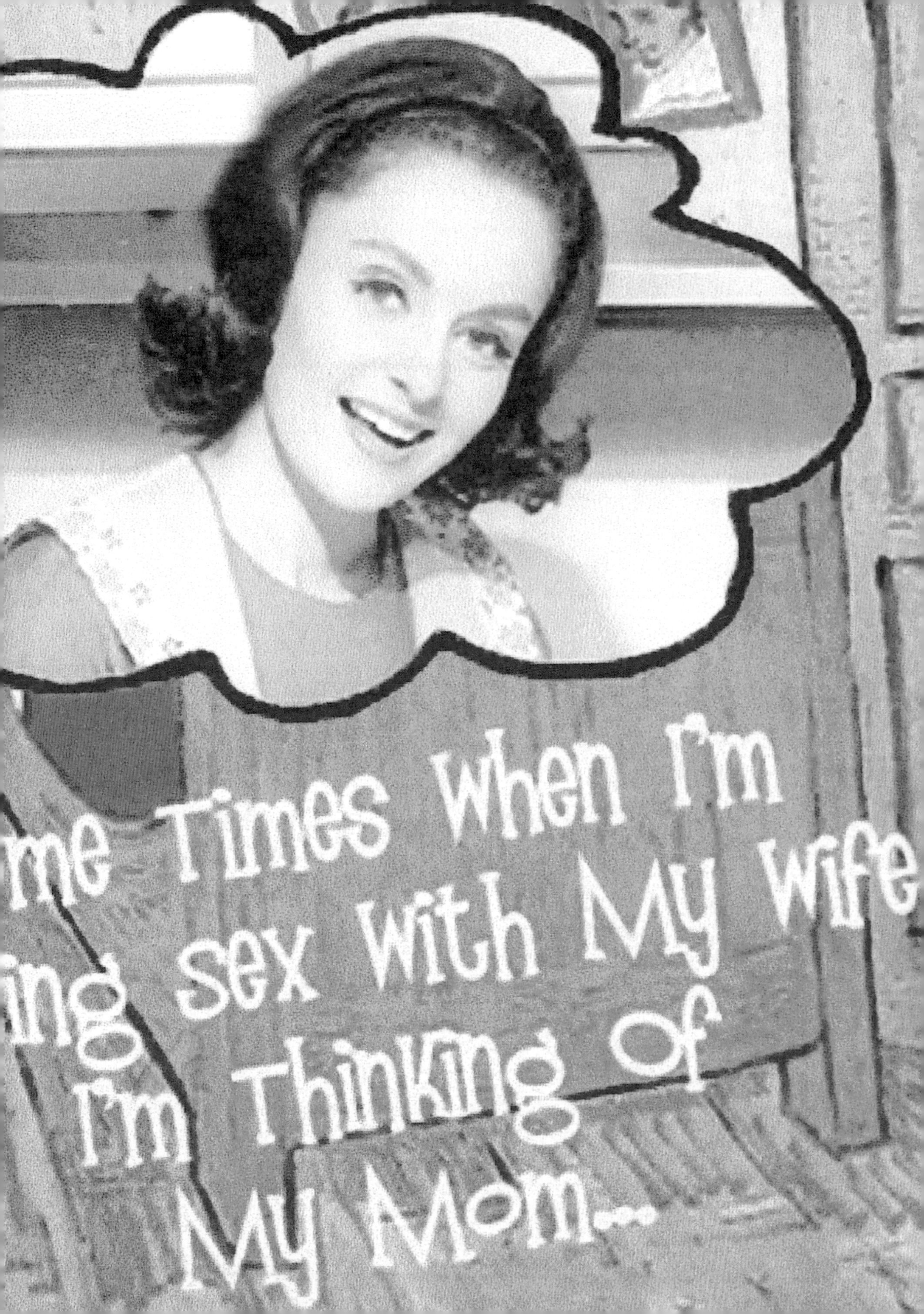
me Times When I'm
ing sex With My Wife
I'm Thinking Of
My Mom...

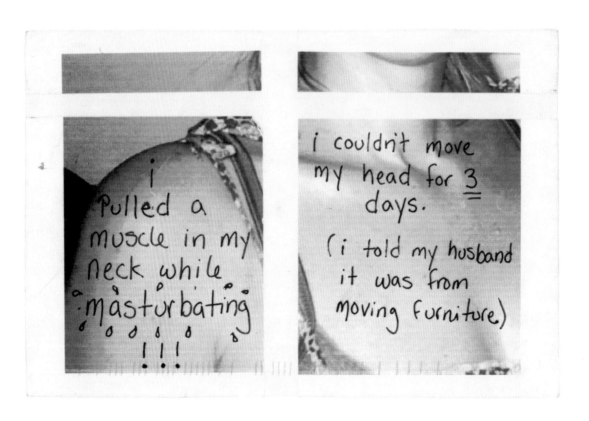

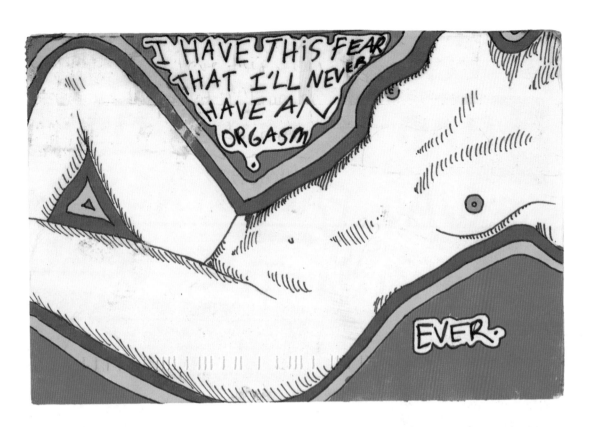

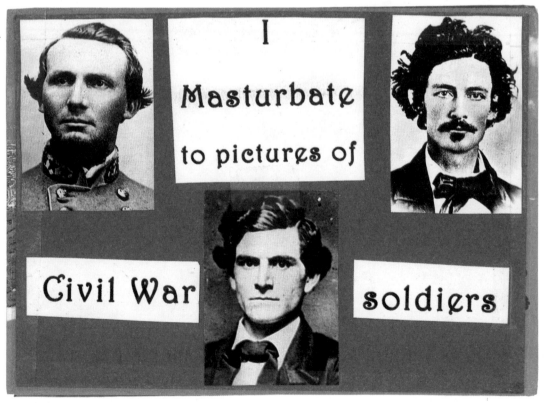

I FEEL REALLY BAD WHEN I HAVE SEXUAL FANTASIES ABOUT THE DEAD.

1943-2001

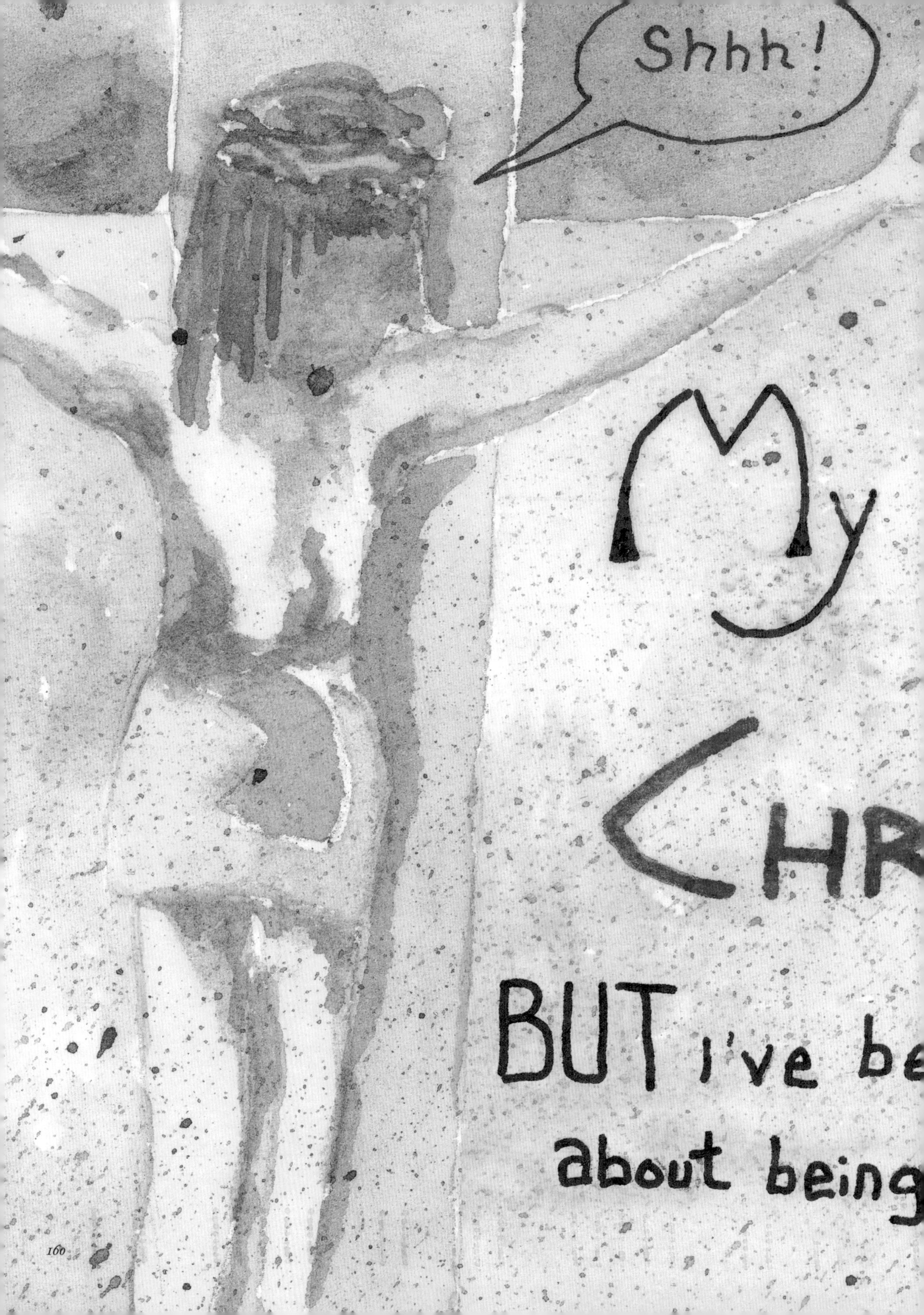
Shhh!
My
CHR
BUT i've be
about being

Grandma

THINKS I'M

ISTIAN

en writing Books
an Atheist!

i
checked
into
a hotel
next to the
train tracks of a
busy Long Island
commuter train line
into new york city. . .
& exhibited myself
nude at night
in the window
when trains passed
I loved it.

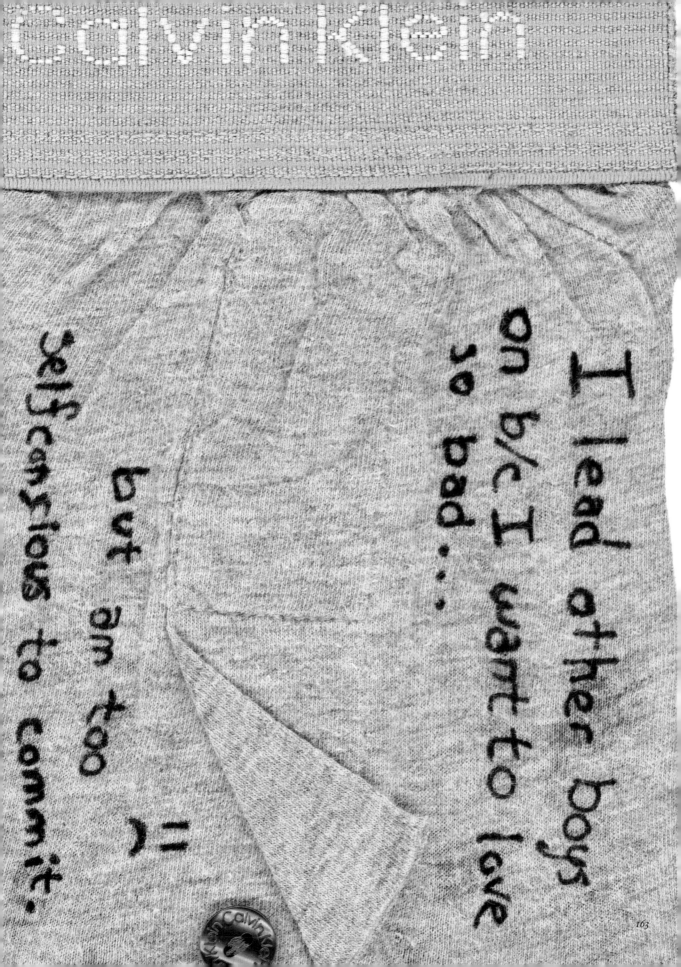

CalvinKlein

I lead other boys
on b/c I want to love
so bad ....

but am too

self conscious to commit.

:-(

163

SOMETIMES I WISH I WAS

A BOY

SO I COULD MAKE OUT WITH GIRLS.

el masterbate

and I hate myself
masterbate

feel Good

I have Sex

to feel wanted

SOMETIMES, I HOPE THE DRUGS WILL TAKE ME AWAY BEFORE THE LONLINESS EVER GETS ITS CHANCE.

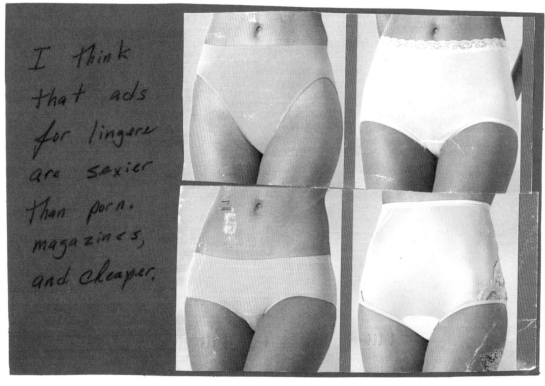

I think that ads for lingere are sexier than porn. magazines, and cheaper.

I NEVER HAD THE PLEASURE OF USING THEM

I've created over a dozen tee-shirts with quotes and photos from obscure films in hopes that someone will recognize them and be the true-blue best friend that I've always dreamed of.

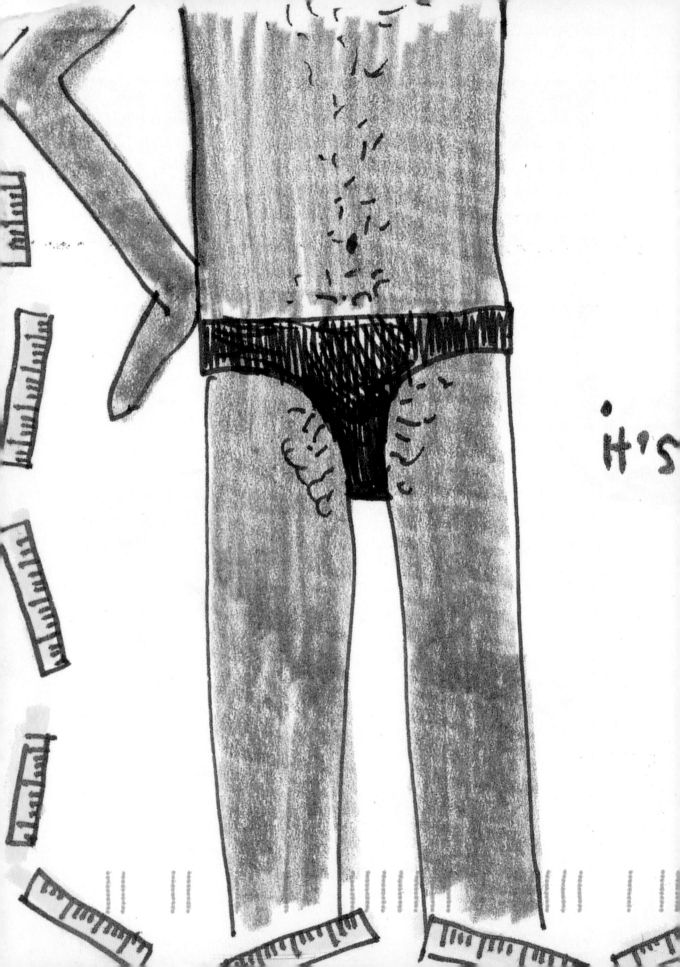

it's

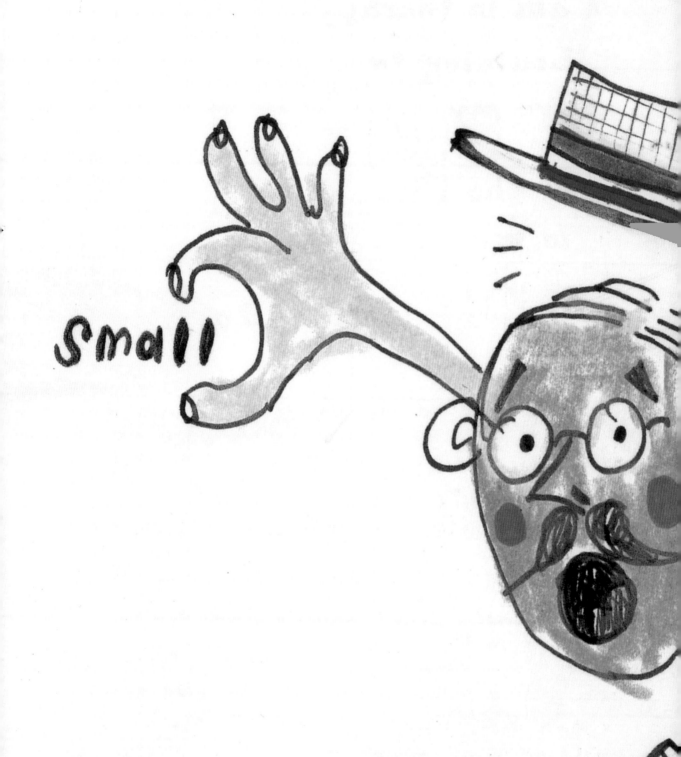

I am in therapy.
Learning to
Love my self
For the First
in my
Life   I am 26.

My neighbor WAS MAKING Too MUCH
Noise. So I CRANKED UP THE VOLUME
ON THe STereO. He CAME over and
GAVE MY TeeNAGe SON SHiT.
I just STOOD THere and NeVER
Stood UP FOR MY SON. I LoVe
MY SoN. I'm SORRY I DiD THiS.
I can'T STOP MY TeeRS as I
WRiTe THiS.   I'm 60 yRs olD
aND will NeVeR FoRGive MYSelF.
I have NeVeR TALKeD To MY SON ABouT THiS

My father was jailed for the rape and molestation of his girlfriend's daughters. He's been there several years. I've always suspected he molested me, as well. But I've never said anything, and I'm scared to find out if my suspicions are true. I'm not sure if my father is the imprisoned one, or if the one imprisoned is ME.

For the first time since I was a baby I am finally HAPPY. I'm 28.

i still beliEVE MY childhood bear is real.

I am in college.

I still talk to her....

when no one is in the room.

I haven't spoken to my dad in 10 years... and it kills me everyday.

In a crowd, (friends, family, strangers) I always wonder which of us will die first.

I used to be pretty.

(Back): *Our one and only photo is hidden behind this postcard . . .*
I love you, I miss you, I want you, I need you, but I couldn't tell.

When I find a picture on the ground, or at school, I put them in my scrap book and write a paragraph and pretend the people in it are my friends.

And I dont feel so ALONE

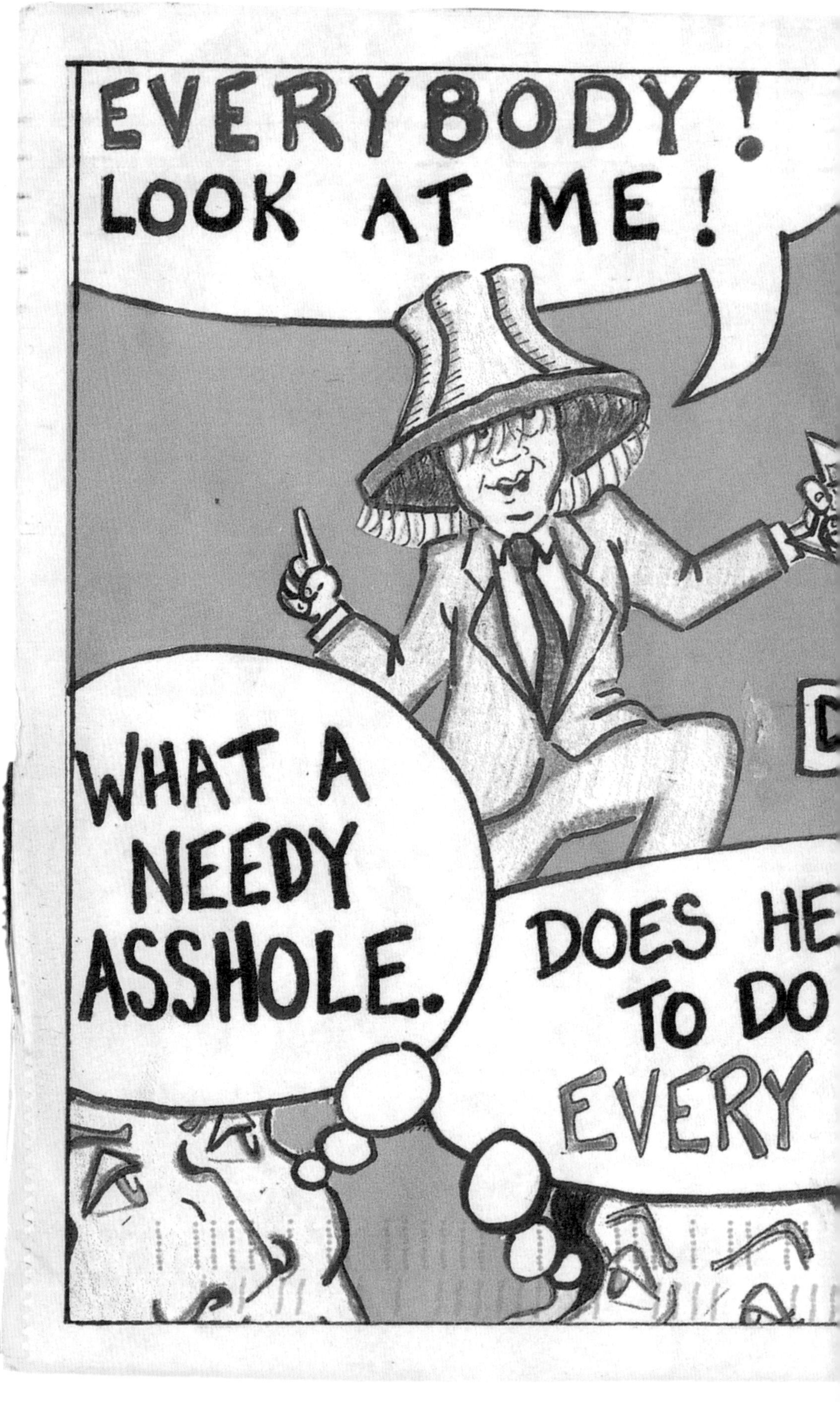
EVERYBODY! LOOK AT ME!
WHAT A NEEDY ASSHOLE.
DOES HE
TO DO
EVERY

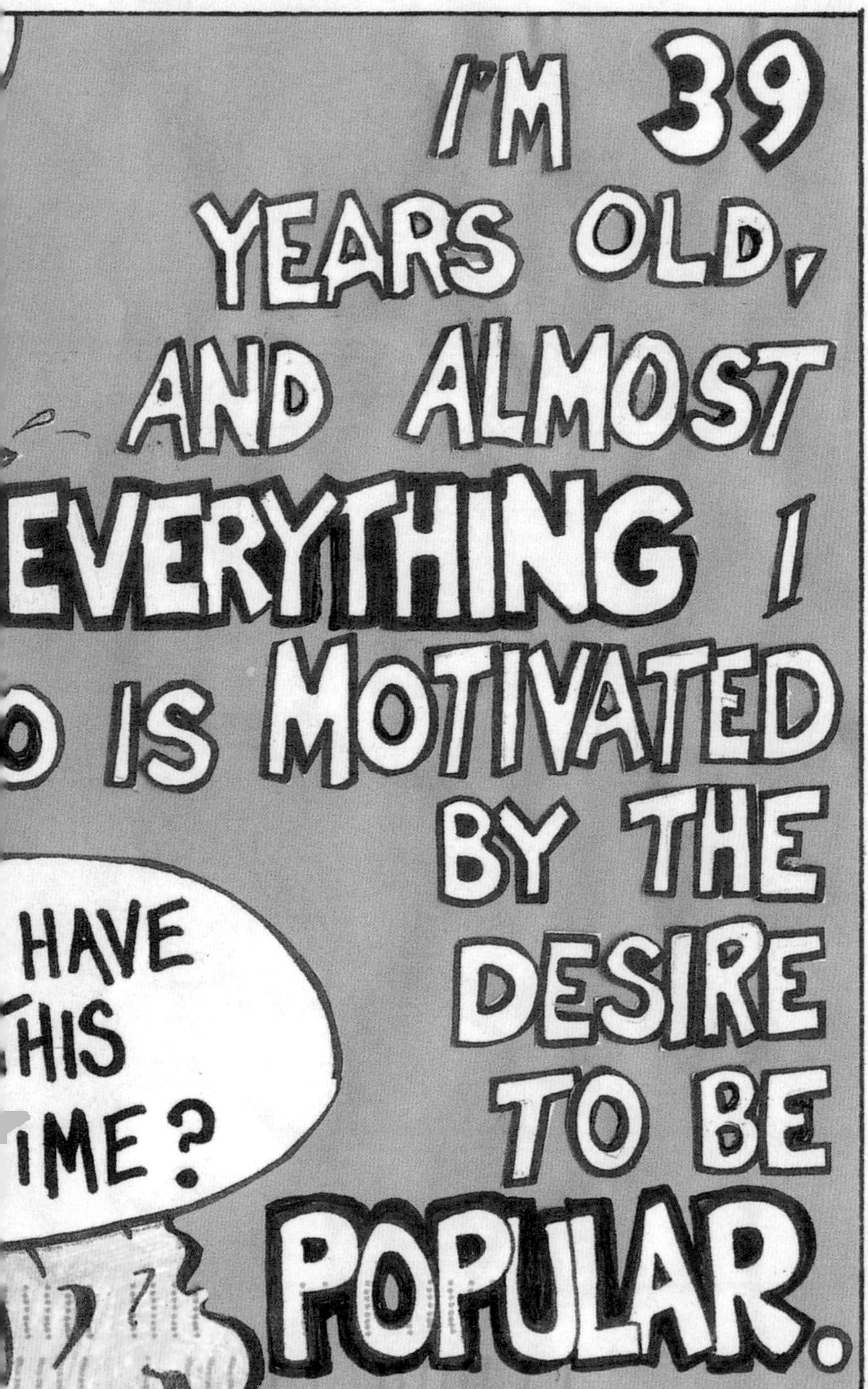
I'M 39 YEARS OLD, AND ALMOST EVERYTHING I
O IS MOTIVATED BY THE DESIRE TO BE POPULAR.
HAVE
HIS
IME?

I actually enjoy being an outcast.

I HATE PEOPLE WHO REMIND ME OF MYSELF.

POSTSECRET
13345 COPPER RIDGE
GERMANTOWN, MD
20874-3154

I MAKE EVERYONE
BELIEVE THAT I
LIKE TO BE

Different,

BUT REALLY I JUST
DON'T KNOW HOW
TO FIT IN.

I WISH I WERE A POPULAR IDIOT
INSTEAD OF A LONELY GENIUS.

$$\int_{-\infty}^{\infty} e^{-st} f(t)\, u(t)\, dt < \heartsuit$$

three years ago my dad died.
one year ago i lost my virginity
to a guy i dated for a month.
if my dad was still alive that
wouldn't have happened.

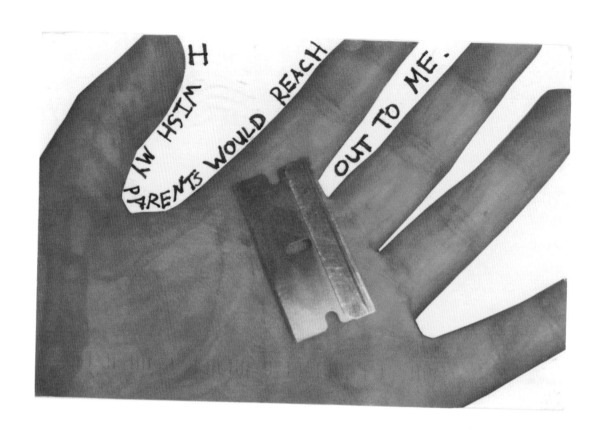

He's running away to follow his dreams...

...Part of me is wishing he fails so we can live out mine...

It hurts so much

NO ONE CAN TURN ME ON MORE THAN MY EIGHTH GRADE BOYFRIEND DID.

I think my actor roommate is ugly and untalented.

I am CONTEMPTUOUS of others so it hurts less when they are INDIFFERENT to me.

186

AT A YOUNG AGE, I WAS RAPED BY A BOY ON THE BACK OF A SCHOOL BUS.

SINCE THEN, I SIT AS CLOSE TO THE FRONT AS I CAN GET.

HEL

my na

I force new acquain

me by my short en

makes me forget

LO
me is

...ances to address

...d name because it

...y past.

"Dear Frank,
After I created my po
be the person with th
I ripped up my postc
start making some ch

tcard, I didn't want to
t secret any longer.
rd and I decided to
anges in my life."

—Texas

I BROKE UP WITH MY

USED TO CALL ME DA

MADE LOVE BECAUSE

WITH A MAN WHO C

WHEN HE FUCKS M

BOYFRIEND WHO
LING WHEN WE
I FELL IN LOVE
LLS ME SLUT

(Back): *I hate billboards so much I have started to vandalize them.*

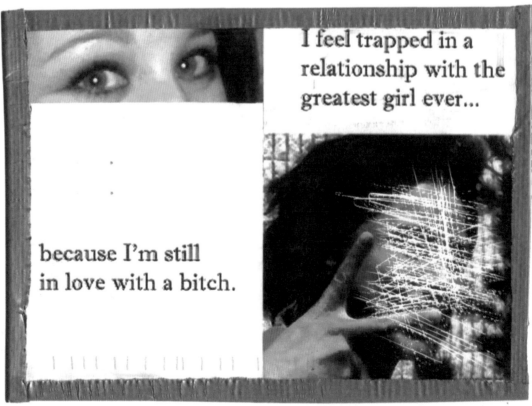

Oc 27 '41   J. Dirky

Hope Sherry

Price: $2.00   No 11 '41Z
         .50   No 18 '41Z
        $2.50
Bill: De 3 '41Z   No 25 '41Z
Renew: De 11 '41Z

Ja3 51   W Benn
Fe   5017 Drexel
        6) Benn
Mr27'51   5017 Drexel
NO 7 '56   J. SEEVER
        4900 BARRY
50 1958
Nov 27 '59 A
Dec 18 '59 Z   J. Aquia
       1009 57th St.

DEC 11 1959 RENEWED

I steal old library cards.
obsessively.

I love the BAND to hide the fact that no one loves ME.

Everyday I type you little Text messages. I tell you I love you. I miss you. Have a wonderful day. Please be careful.

But I don't send them. I know I'm not supposed to.

But I hope that somehow, You know...

I MISS YOU...
I WISH YOU
WOULD CALL...

I am unable to share my secret, but know this; the most expensive drink you will ever taste is free alcohol.

i wish
i were
still
innocent.

i
lost
my
virginity
last
week

but i don't feel any different

I JOINED BECAUSE I WAS PATRIOTIC. BUT SINCE THEY SUCCEEDED IN CONVINCING ME MY LIFE IS WORTHLESS, I'M JUST HOPING I GET SHOT.

SUICIDAL SOLDIER

i miss the good ol'days

DKGFJAKEWRNRNADFDDLKJADGFIEORJYGOIAHGLKADN
OIUJTAOIREUJTOAIEJGADGADKNGFADLKGFFDLKJAGFDL
LKIJFDGOIUAHARETOIUHERTOIAHEGTOIEHRTOIHAETRC
IZBVIMDALKGJFLKGLAKDJGFKJFGAOIEWUJRTOIOIQOIW
VIETRNEVERWOIEPPALKGCPCPCPCIJHAETKJEWJAIEJREY
ERKJANKGFLIKEDJDAOIJRETPIAJETRLIHADLGUHLGAIUHO
ATGIUHATRPUAYOURPIUHANMNZVCKJHADSOGFUREWP
ASMADSM,NFADUHPOETRY,EWOUTROIHWLIJKALJKZLJK
AKJNDSKJNDGFAFDLJHGFDPIUEHRTPIUEIUHALUJHEIUH
DFLJGKJNAMNZVCMNCBMNADOIHAGLKJHERTIUHATREI
RUTUAUAYDIFUAHGDYADSFLKJHAGYALKJHGAYALKHG
ASDFHJLADSFHLKJQEUTRIPOQUTREIPQETRUIPOQTREUQF
HGLKJADJKNMZNVCMNZXCMVNXMVCNOIUJADKJHGFDK
GFJHADJGHEIRUHTAEOIUTRHANM,ZNCVMNCXZVNMBCX
LKJHADGFLKJHDLKJGHNDFAKNAMNZCXVMNARDSKIHH
HOUAHDTLKJREHLKJAMNZVCXKJHADLKJFHAGFDJHFDGI
DFGJHADGFIUEHRTGIUANMZNADKGALJHADKJHDGFIUHO
GLUIHARIUHGEAKJNHADJNVNCMXZLHUALUAHRDGIUHA
FHDFLKJGHADLKJGHAEOIUYEATRKJHALKJHHGFSRYUYF
CTDTDYTYTHYASDFGHWERTYOIYHFVDECGBJHGYTFKYU
HLKJAHGIUAHENFGJANHGFDIUAHETRJNBADFJGHADKJG
VUUAUBSWUEHGTRKIAREKJAHDGNDXHXIARGAUNSIAUF
CVKJHDSAIUHWEURHATIUYHTIUIUHGAHWQWEIUQWEQK
XZXHZIUHSEIUHSDFIUHEIKUGTEIUREDPLDFOKDSGMABI
JEJHRGOIHAGOIHADGOIHREOITHTEOIHAKDKJNZMNZXCM
AKHAJHAKZXCBIUHESIUHWETIUYWIQIUQIUEWHRATOUF
KJAGJHAMNBZCOIUHUJGUYUGIOAKUGKIUYGUYTFTRDW
YTYUJ8JTHGFYYRRRYGNIMKMOOKLOKOJIJINUBUBUYBY
CFTVYBBKBJHGFTFYTRDFHNVJBHGKNBHKJBHKVJGFCFCI
GLJKBKJBHUYVYTKJVKLOLKLKUYKIUYTFYTFDRDRTDKV
BGYTTRDCKIYTFGKHGBYTKUHKUKUYFKFRTDJHGDSKH
GADGFLIJADKLJGADKJFGAOIUWRETIOUATREKJMNZCXV

when i eat, i feel like a failure.

(French): *I hate every part of my body (except my hands).*

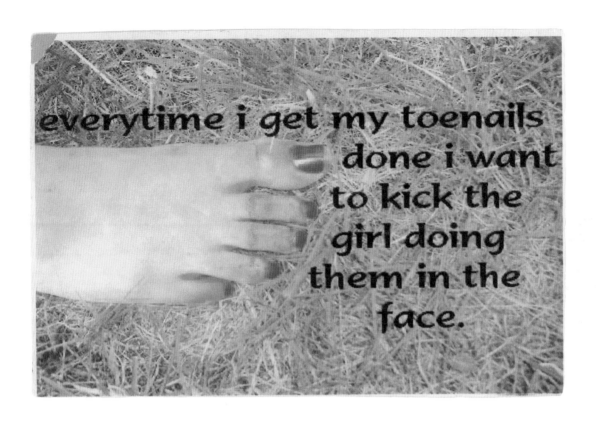

everytime i get my toenails done i want to kick the girl doing them in the face.

i know it really stinks. but i like the smell of my own poop.

the medication is not enough
to make me forget
what he did to me...
if i see him again
i will kill him to save
the others

i truly think that judgement day is NEAR

but people take it as a joke

Sometimes I romanticize my roots (more "ethnic," more blue collar ....) to be more interesting at chic cocktail parties.

I'm a good liar.

I still haven't told my father that I have the same disease that killed my mother.

COMPASSION•TRUST• •LOVE•JOY•

guilt • pain • Sadness • purple • blood •

black • blue • rape • hit • scream • silence

AND HE NEVER WILL•AND HE NEVER WILL•AND HE NEVER WILL

I
LOVE My HUSband
because he's the only
MAN I've been
with who hasn't
hurt my body
with
Violence

AND HE NEVER WILL•AND HE NEVER WILL

I'm with
the first person
I've ever been able
to truly trust.

He is the only
person I have
ever cheated
on!

I wish I was white.

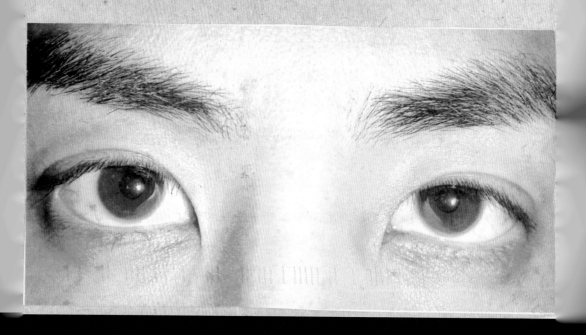

I'M AFRAID
to ANSWER THE

TELEPHONE

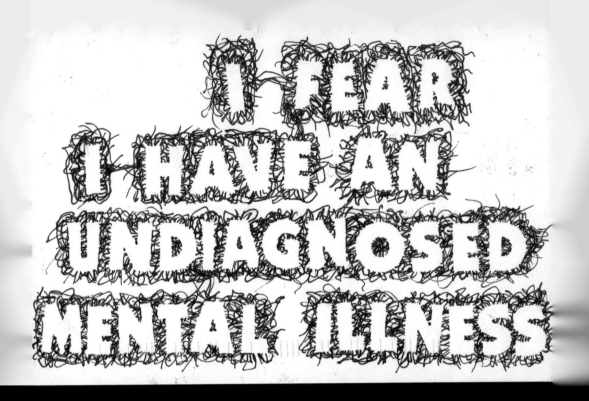

I FEAR
I HAVE AN
UNDIAGNOSED
MENTAL ILLNESS

I feel ugly because
I'm half-black, half-white.

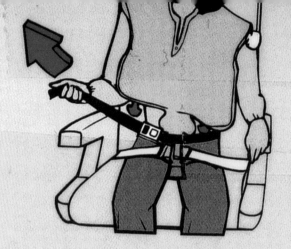

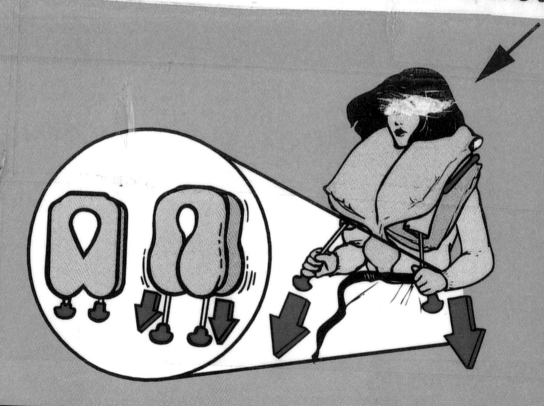

I wanted the plane to crash so I wou

dn't have to miss him anymore.

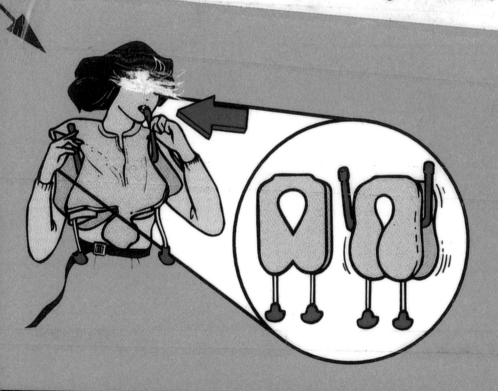

My hands
shake as I
mail this.

(I was so wrong.)

postsecret
13345 copper ridge
                    Rd
Germantown, Maryland
           20874-3454

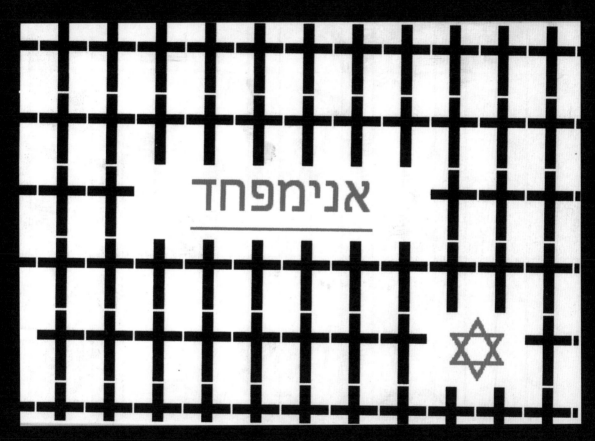

(Hebrew): *I'm afraid*

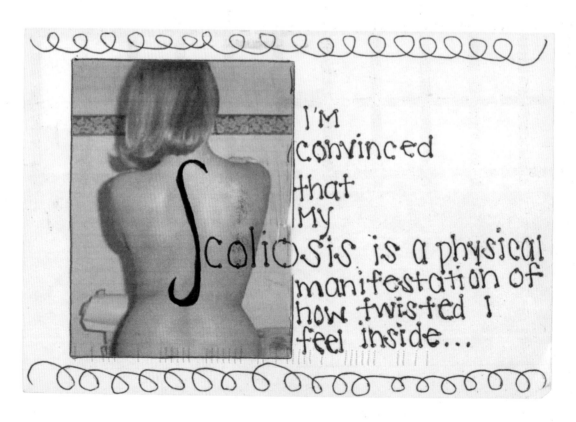

she isn't

YOUTHS

Sometimes I think my fiancé isn't

THE ONE

Most people believe
that I should hate him
most for hurting me.

But I don't.

I hate him *most*
for making me think
I deserved it.

I hope he burns in
HELL.

Christ

Christ

CHRIST

CHRIST

I
am
a
Southern Baptist Pastor'sWife.
No
one
knows
that
I do
not
believe
in
God.

I was Seven Years old the **first** time I attempted SUICIDE thank you

I write the same thing on all of my thank you notes, and I worry that my reletives will compare them and find out.

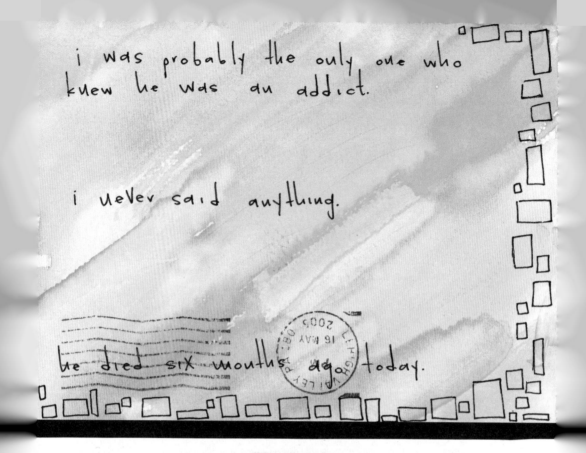

i was probably the only one who knew he was an addict.

i never said anything.

he died six months ago today.

SOMETIMES WHEN I DO CHINESE TAKEOUT, I ORDER FOR 2 PEOPLE SO I WON'T LOOK LIKE A FAT, LONELY LOSER.

Then I eat it all.

... I want to die ......

.... a hero

i still suck
my thumb)
i'm 18.

Once I was asked by a doctor

if I was hearing voices.

The voice inside my head shouted:

TELL HIM NO!

WHEN I LISTEN TO MY PATIENTS

ALL I CAN THINK ABOUT IS HOW

I DRUG THAT RAZOR ACROSS MY

.KIN, TOO...

AND HOW MUCH I MISS IT.

TERN UNION

TELEGRAM

W. P. MARSHALL, PRESIDENT

1213 (7-58)

CHARGE TO THE ACCOUNT OF

TIME FILED

are hereby agreed to

I ONCE PLANNED

Destination

TO KILL MY

MOTHER

and address (For reference)

Sender's telephone number

This Jackass at my
school died.
Kind of happy. I'm
don't
of happy that I
have to see him one
more.

i have to shave
my TOES...(i am
a woman...)

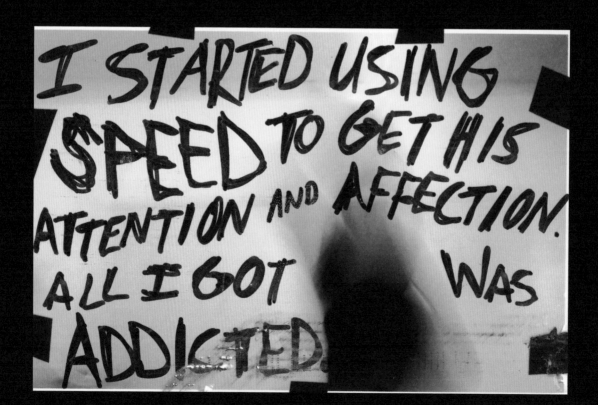

I STARTED USING
$PEED TO GET HIS
ATTENTION AND AFFECTION.
ALL I GOT WAS
ADDICTED.

MY MOM
KILLED MY
DAD,
LONG BEFORE
HE KILLED
HIMSELF.

I LOVE
TO PEE
WHEN
I'M
SWIMMING

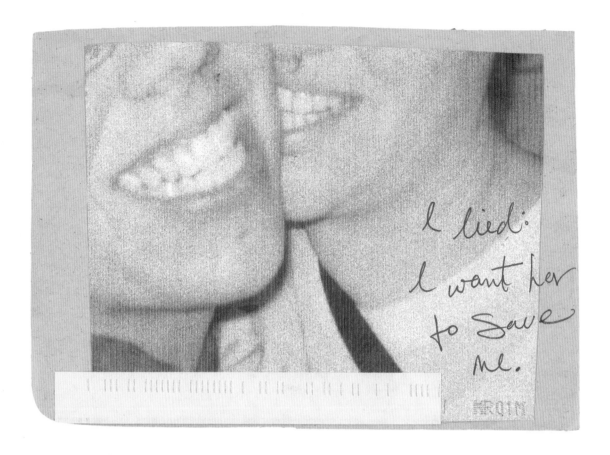

I lied:
I want her
to save
me.

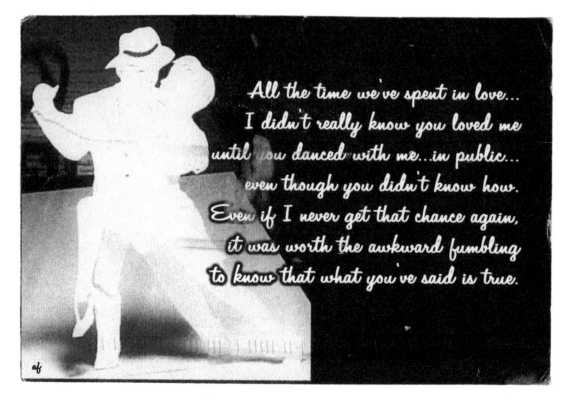

All the time we've spent in love...
I didn't really know you loved me
until you danced with me...in public...
even though you didn't know how.
Even if I never get that chance again,
it was worth the awkward fumbling
to know that what you've said is true.

I THINK
I AM
IN LOVE.
AND I DON'T
KNOW IF I
WANT TO BE.
I AM KIND
OF SCARED.

I'm still in love with her.

I hope she reads this,
and recognizes my handwriting.

this is also my last try.

"Dear Frank,
I have made six postcards
afraid to tell the one pers
my boyfriend. This morni
but instead I left them on
head while he was sleeping
at my office and asked me
I said yes."

all with secrets that I was

n I tell everything to,

g I planned to mail them,

the pillow next to his

Ten minutes ago he arrived

to marry him.

—Canada

I'm Falling
For you...

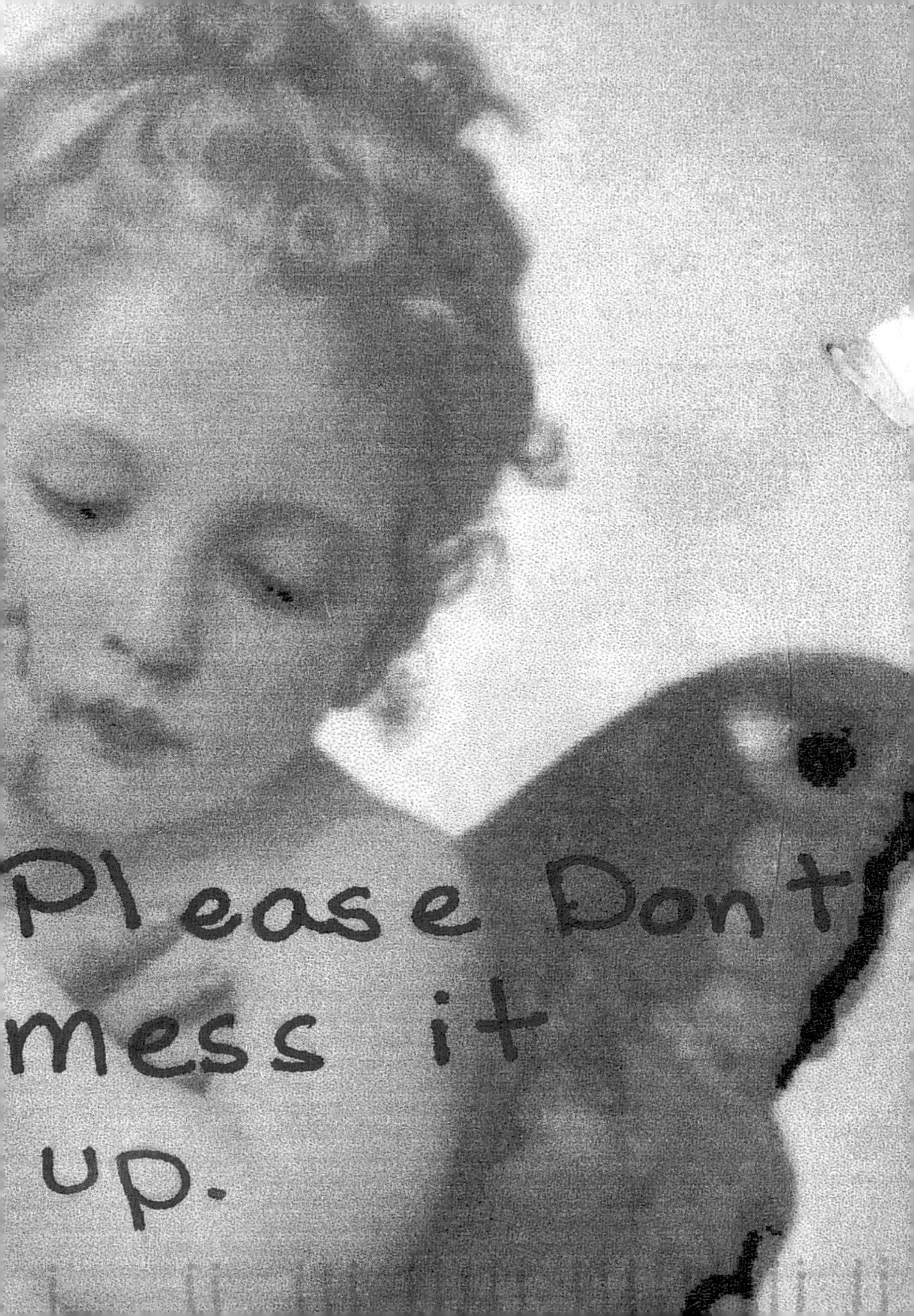
Please Dont
mess it
up.

I'm known as the "funny" one,   but I d

It's because I fear feeling their sadness.

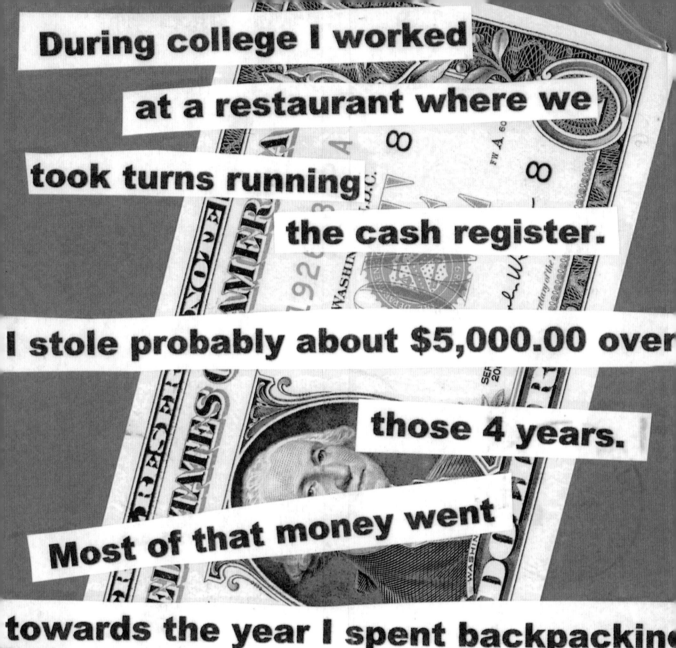

During college I worked

at a restaurant where we

took turns running

the cash register.

I stole probably about $5,000.00 over

those 4 years.

Most of that money went

towards the year I spent backpacking

around Europe.

I had a great time.

I only smoke
Pall Mall Cigarettes
so I can
remember you
forty times
a day...

THE NIGHTS I SLEEP
THE BEST
I DREAM ABOUT
BEING SHOT

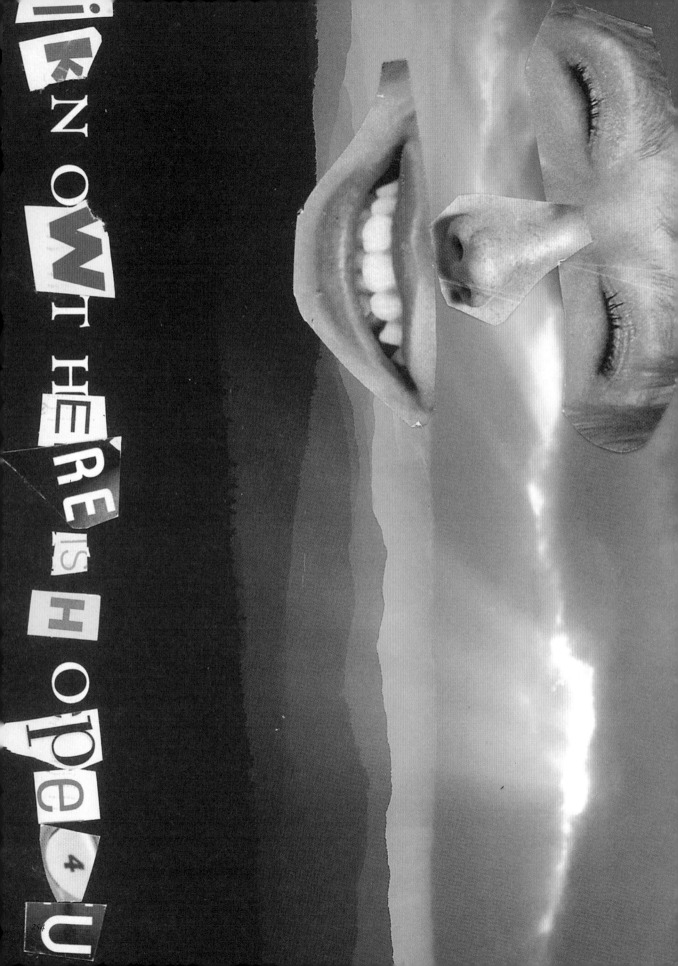

i was only
trying to hurt
myself as
much as i
hurt
him.

i am so sorry ... him.

i'm afraid of
women who wear
capri pants

(Back): *I burn my father's porn when he's not home.*

I STOLE YOUR DUCK AND TOOK HIM TO SAN FRANCISCO

the night he died he tried to call me...when I saw it was him, I didnt answer.

I wish I would have left the mask **ON**.

When I go shopping, I pretend I can buy a boyfriend...

... In the UNDERWEAR section! :)

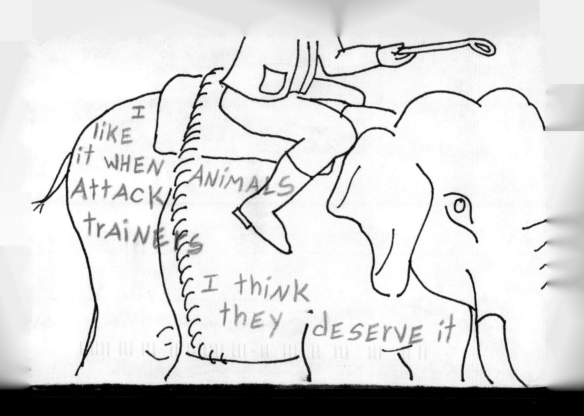

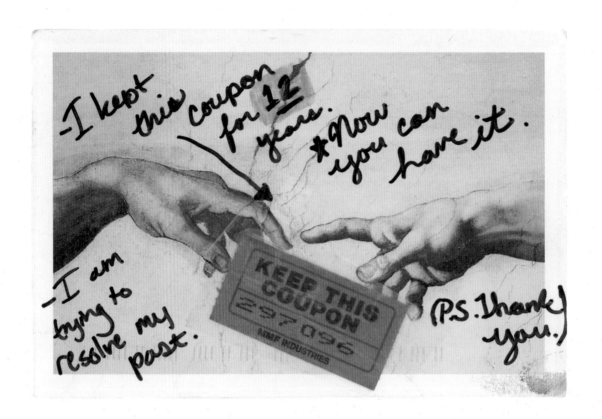

I need to change.

I'm getting a tattoo about

♥ LOVE ♥

To cover a scar that reminds me of just how much I used to

× HATE ×

myself.

I still wonder
what life would be like
if I'd just
had the courage
to tell her

We haven't spoken in 5 years and I'm happily married

1979.
FOURTH GRADE LUNCH
CONFRONTED BY BU
I HASTILY BROK
WONDER
ROUTINE, HOPIN
THE BIG GOO
BUT CONSIDERIN
SCRAWNY RUNT
it DIDN'T GO DOW

ERIOD.

LLIES,

INTO A

WOMAN

to FRIGHTEN

NS OFF.

I WAS A

OF A BOY

too WELL.

gave my vegetarian sister a meal with beef

I change my hair so often to make up for the fact that I won't be able to change who I am.

I LOVE YOU SO MUCH BUT CAN'T TELL YOU!!!

I LEAVE poetry IN LIBRARY BOOKS.

I intentionally make myself nearly a half an hour late to work every morning so I can ride the bus with the hot bus driver, in hopes that we may make eye contact in the rear view mirror and perhaps start a conversation. I think up hun- dreds of opening lines as I let buses pass me by, but when he opens the doors and smiles brightly and looks at me with his beautiful sparkling blue eyes I find myself tongue twisted. I end up burying my head inside a book. Maybe he'll read this someday......

I TRASHED MY PARENTS
HOUSE TO LOOK LIKE I HAD
HAD A PARTY WHILE THEY WERE
OUT OF TOWN...

I ...SO MY MOM WOULD THINK
I HAD FRIENDS:

Psst, Here's a secret...
Your last mortal thought
will be, "why did I take
so many days - just like
today - for granted?"

I know that sending in a stupid postcard to share a secret
with a bunch of strangers won't do a damn thing to change
the daily loneliness and unhappiness in my life.

And I sent this anyway.

I bought a bunch of postcard Stamps to use for Post Secret but I used them to write to My friends instead.

:)

I like to believe that whenever a painful secret ends its trip to my mailbox, a much longer personal journey of healing is beginning—for all of us.

—Frank

SHARE A SECRET

You are invited to anonymously contribute a secret to a group
art project. Your secret can be a regret, fear, betrayal, desire,
confession or childhood humiliation. Reveal *anything* - as long
as it is true and you have never shared it with anyone before.

Steps:
    Take a postcard, or two.
    Tell your secret anonymously.
    Stamp and mail the postcard.

Tips:
    Be brief – the fewer words used the better.
    Be legible – use big, clear and bold lettering.
    Be creative – let the postcard be your canvas.

SEE A SECRET
www.postsecret.com

PostSecret
13345 Copper Ridge Rd
Germantown, Maryland
20874-3454